Holgersonj@aol.com W9-DAT-689

Broken Borders
poems

Broken Borders
poems

John L. Holgerson

Wasteland Press

www.wastelandpress.net
Shelbyville, KY USA

Broken Borders
by John L. Holgerson

First Printing – January 2012
ISBN: 978-1-60047-675-4
Cover Painting: Adrien-Louis Demont (French 1851-1928)
Don Quixote 1893 oil on canvas 111.0 x 156.0 cm
National Gallery of Victoria, Melbourne (Purchased 1893)
Back cover photograph by Bill Holgerson

Printed in the U.S.A.

0   1   2   3   4   5   6   7   8   9   10   11

One needs a place in which to play and one must play with language to engage a place at all in poetry...I'm not much interested in unpopulated landscapes.

John Matthias

Contents

Part II Early Views

Part III At the Next Frontier

Acknowledgments

About the Author

The Landscape of the Heart

These poems were written in Indiana, Massachusetts, London, England, Athens, Greece, and on the Greek islands of Hydra and Rhodes. A few of them were born in one country, grew up in a second and found maturity in a third. The fact that these poems had their births in various locations is in geographic harmony with the theme of this volume: the diverse landscape of the heart.

That landscape is made up of broad and varied territories. While these territories define, they can also limit. We know this and, over time, accept the boundaries that have been drawn. Yet, the urge to break these borders and expand the landscape never dissipates completely; even though we know the price can be high for what we leave behind in a well-established and comfortable province.

Many of these territories have natural borders. Others we ourselves carve out or are etched for us. Some we hold as open range; some cannot–should not–have trespassers. On occasion, though, we invite a select few to come and share all the different views.

Thank you, Gentle Reader, for accepting the invitation.

I.

Old and New Territories

Dancing Desperado

When music plays, you dance.
Across the room, in the street,
you glide. An escaped kite
rising on crescendo currents,
tugging slave to string of song.

When music plays, you sing
in memory of poems you wrote
when your greed for love
was a disease. I am immune,
an outlaw from such need.

When music plays, I fear
all excuses and delays.
My poems are yours for the asking,
even the ones written
for someone else's seduction.

Perform your ballet of prayer
without pirouette or passion.
You are a desperado too.
And I wait for you to dance
for me, when music plays.

Fatal Beauty

All her lovers were poor explorers
History books will so record
Though they combed her hair
and mapped her body
her naked beauty they ignored.

They chartered her deepest curves
They named her every part
Though they planted flags
and cried out commands
she never gave up her heart.

They thought they had won her
She kissed all their tears
Though they were so wrong
and sucked so dry
their souls were her souvenirs.

All her lovers she did conquer
She trapped them hopelessly
Though she did warn them
and her new explorers
who wait their turn so patiently.

He and She at the Restaurant

They sat at the outdoor table
not seeing the storm coming
He did not order
She did

Their talk was pillow soft
lovers barely twenty
He did not speak much
She did

"That's fine for the tenth time
but what about the long term?"
He did not answer
She did

"I don't feel like eating."
She pushed her plate away
He did not move
She did

She left her chair askew
her face wet and hot
She said good-bye and walked
He did not

When love isn't hungry
it eats you whole.

On the First Anniversary of the Night the Red Sox Won the World Series (October 25, 2005)

I thought of you
tonight

watching the moon

an ashen buoy
amid charcoal clouds cruising
on an indifferent
onyx ocean

hearing Boston bats

ancient curses crushing
in the quiet bridging our words
mine spoken diffidently
or not at all

savoring the talk

the coy compliment
a familiar trespasser
wanting not to be a
perfect gentleman

standing shoeless

a grey Greek beach
ribbed with broken rocks
shattered smaller than
a silent heart

I thought of you
tonight

Gift of Ribbon

Before us
brave paladins brought ribbons
and vernal bouquets to maidens fair.
Tenderness must be bartered.

Near us
on playgrounds at twilight
giggling children conspire
to hold night in abeyance.
Defeated, they saunter home
to sleep with their secrets
to sleep with their wonders.

Far from us
the violated moon
czaress of the seas
floats roughly across
the rocket scarred sky
as self-ordained kings
sit in fear

mesmerized by moonlight
shining on scythes
raised over them
by mutinous victims
with deceit etched
in their smiling eyes.

Around us
hunters stand watching
you move between them
order to order
table to table
harvesting rows

of empty glasses growing
thick on formica fields.

And who are these hunters
laughing by your side?
Exiled kings skilled
in tyranny of the heart?
Bold rebels seizing subtly
your style and grace?

Love only the children of dusk.
They would share their secrets.
They would share their wonders.

Between us
this gossamer ribbon of words
does not tie or bind
your yesterdays or tomorrows
to any of mine.

As knights errant
once gave gifts of ribbon
I would bring thee poems
and the first flowers
of a summer rain.

Fair Warning

Do not go so unarmed
among the smiling hunters
Do not listen
to the clever lures
whispered from behind
blinds of bravado

They are the grass and dirt
hiding
the deceptive snare
the spiked pit
the heart-crushing trap

Do not travel so surely
among the jealous jailers
Do not seek out
their dark shelters
secluded in a
tower torture chamber

They are the lairs and havens
harboring
the branding iron
the sacrificial altar
the peanut-strewn cage

Do not stroll so easily
among the unknown poets
Do not trust us
to repair your heart
We will shackle it
with chains of verse

We are the cruelest jailers
We are the keenest hunters

I've stood in some cold cathedrals

I've stood in some cold cathedrals
where sun-soaked stained-glass windows
shower a spot-light of rainbows
on the Dove's empty nest
resting in ornate marble meadows.

Here is my soul to tame
Let it hear Your voice
Let it hear You call me
by my only real name.

Unconvinced by cathedrals
where the Dove was not at home,
I visited a saint's rotting relics
hidden from the Huns
in the sacred catacombs.

Carved on a torch-lit wall
with a sprig of my sins in its beak,
the Dove kept watch over a virgin
burning at the stake
on a cold, stony mountain peak.

Here is my soul to tame
Let it hear Your voice
Let it hear You call me
by my only real name.

My pilgrimage unfinished,
I fled the bowels of martyrdom
to climb the steep mountain's side;
mud shackles round my ankles,
filthy fingertips bloodied numb.

On top, amid old pines, a monastery
stands forlorn in the virgin's honor.
A charcoal bearded monk bathed me,
frowned when I asked
why no man had won her.

Here is my soul to tame
Let it hear Your voice
Let it hear You call me
by my only real name.

Clothed in a monk's old, tattered habit,
I saw the Dove as He hovered
high in the unbroken azure sky,
the feathers of His world-weary wings
from the warm, narrow beds of His lovers.

Evangelismós

At sunset, lights lace the harbor
Men and women stroll the waterfront
eating ice cream cones
broken hearts hidden
among dissolving firework flashes
Broken hearts elsewhere forgotten
on this night of laughter without tears.

Night in Rhodes

the sky melts
blue to indigo
you want to dip
your pen in it
to write all
antiquity
has left for you
to say

Prayer for a Basketball Player

for Justin

May the floor of your life
be the hardwood of the court:
Solid, even, with a goal at its end.
May you always see it well
and avoid the out of bounds.

May you always realize
the assists you give to others
help you win this game
more than the goals
you score for yourself.

May you always remember
team play is required
as you rarely win this game alone.
Sharing the rock with others
makes everyone's game better.

May you never be intentionally fouled.
If you are, do not foul in return.
Raise your hand for the fouls you commit,
doing that in this life means
not fouling out of the next.

May you always remember
good deeds are like free throws.
They cost you nothing and,
when you make them,
they add points to your score.

May all you try
never be an air ball
or bricked off the rim.
Follow your shots, rebound well,
put the ball back in.

May you always have the open shot
in everything you do.
May all those shots be followed
by the soft, silent swish
that means so much to you.

In the hallway
for Alissa

Invoked apparitions
of your childhood
parade toward me
in the hallway

a smiling toddler
with braided hair
next to a deeply tanned
pony-tailed teenager

the face of innocence
never disappointed
asleep on a blue pillow
melds into

resignation distilled
from the never timely
deaths of Santa Claus
and Sandy the candy elf.

Skinny legs
in cutoff jeans
assume length and shape
in dungaree skirts

morphing to false modesty
in pants belonging
to unloved, rarely worn
gray-stripped business suits.

These phantoms appear
in a mob of memories
as I stand staring
eyes wide shut

in the doorway
of your old room
in a house grown silent
of children's laughter.

On the Birthdays of My Daughter and Son

When you were small

My hair was wavy and brown
My step was quick and very sure
My skin, like yours, had no wrinkles at all

when you were small

My strength was rock steady
My vision sharp and far too clear
My hand held onto yours; you could not fall

when you were small

My answers went undoubted
My requests unchallenged
My wisdom had no limit, a high endless wall

when you were small

My gifts came wrapped in Xs and Os
My valentines in lace-edged crayon
My ardent heart held yours freely in thrall

when you were small

Robin, at Christmas

Snow falls on the roads
leading from this city.
The roads I nearly took
when I thought cold
froze grace and beauty.

With your touch and smile,
all God has made I hold.
Grace and beauty thaw
with words free from guile.
Snow obliterates the roads.

So we are all sitting

for John Matthias

So we are all sitting
in this classroom
it was the Rolling Stones
"Paint It Black" sixties
bell-bottomed jeans or corduroys
beads and long hair
(but not down the back)

It was Notre Dame
Four years of male bonding
with only St. Mary's women on campus
(Rally Sons of Notre Dame
what though the odds be great or small)
We were there-Strangers
Year Two-Semester Two-Day One

The professor walks in
bell-bottomed corduroys
beard and long hair
(but not down the back)
He looks around
some sort of semi-smile
on his face.

He knows we know
it is his first or second class
(but it will not be
a second-class class)
He focuses on no one
on everyone

He sits on the corner
of his desk
corduroy bell-bottoms
exposing boots with
made-for-walking heels
And he opens this book
Babette Deutsch *On Poetry*

turns it face down
on his desk
like he knows
some secret we don't
which he does but
we don't know that then
not til many lines later

when it dawns on me
in the midst of
feeding my head
writing some stanza
in a courtroom
with a client waiting
for the jury's verdict.

Courtroom of Love

I am waiting
for my case to be called
out of the backlog
of nonsuits and defaults
in the courtroom of love

Excuses paper-clipped
to its docket
like parking tickets
under a towed car's
windshield wiper

Too afraid to face
the punishment
for cracking walls
in the chambers of the heart,
I chose not to appear

leaving angry women
to gather in a small group
in the hallways of justice
seeking something else
more painful for me

Picked up by their
under the covers agent,
handcuffed, held without bail,
I'm in the bulletproof dock
in the courtroom of love

The judge comes out
takes the bench
turns to me
and she smiles
the same way

Pontius Pilot smiled
at the carpenter's son
as he freed Barabbas
and issued the order
for another cross

I cannot love you now

I cannot love you now
I could not have loved you then

when the Jefferson Starship
was just an Airplane
when Eric Clapton was Cream
and Neil Young was Shakey

during the Summer of Love
during the short days of JFK
and long nights of Vietnam

I cannot love you now
I could not have loved you then

in a Woodstock field of sex and drugs
in the diplomatic waters of the Bay of Pigs
in the haters' heat of a Mississippi night

on a taken seat in a Montgomery bus
on a rocket ship in outer space
on the virgin surface of the moon

I cannot love you then
I could have loved you now

Not Missing Anything

The train has left the station
I heard its engine roar
It is not going anywhere
I have not been before.

To A Married Woman

The invitation extended
A reply not required
Silence the harbinger
for regretted refusal
and anticipated acceptance
held in mutual abeyance
as we enter Heavens' rodeo
from the Bridge of Details:
Your turn to catch a star
My turn to lasso the moon.

From November, To June

Outside my window
down the paved road
bare branches
hover over
thinning brown grass
the promise of peonies
long past

Outside your window
up the paved road
green leaves
rustle on
budding red maples
the vows of violets
pure, supple

My blue want for you
an unseen side road
buried beneath
falling words
disengaged
as crude cryptic verse
smudges the page.

Into the Garden

When he asked
she brought him
into the garden
through a rusted iron gate

She took him
from his oak desk
and stacked books
with broken bindings

from his brass bed
of warm rumpled sheets
where familiar flesh slept
in wrinkled moonlight

In the garden
she showed him
where she laid with her husband
among the lilacs and the lilies

she showed him
where she played with her lover
beneath the wizened willows
stooped with moss

During his time with her
he wanted to be either
knowing he could be neither
And when he realized

he was the alibi for one
the scapegoat for the other
he made her escort him
from the garden

back to his oak desk
and stacked books
with rotting bindings
covered in uncaring dust

back to his brass bed
where cold pinpoints of starlight
shimmer in the flat moonlight
on neatly turned sheets.

Failure

You not loving me
did not compel me

to draw the curtains
across my windows

or mutter obscenities
under my breath

It was my inability
to seduce you

with flowers and poems
that made me a recluse

Broken Glass

This wanting you
is the grinding
of broken glass
in my soul

I miss the nights
in the monastery
where the only pain
contemplated

was in the Master's eyes
when caught
in a weak prayer
thinking of you

Gift

This gift of silence
you have given me
(or is it a curse)

spreads like fog
from your town
to my city

through the forests
marking the trees
with angry symbols

stunning songbirds
so they plummet quietly
from their perches

descending on
backyard barbeques
of strangers and friends

forcing them to hide
their scared unfed children
behind locked cellar doors

then cloaks my house
clouds my views
curls down my chimney

seeps through
the broken seals
of windows and doors

enshrouds me
while you hold
your voice captive

and this gift
that cannot be exchanged
the ransom to be paid

Out of Order

Are we not
today's perfect people

broken

with parts
not in stock

due to
the high demand
for repair

the way it was then
for Charles Bukowski

Buk,
you once said
you wouldn't drive
backwards to New York
to live again with any
of the beautiful women
from your past

What bullshit, Hank
the way it was then
the first lonely moment
you'd have driven there
backwards
without brakes
or a rearview mirror

had any one of them still
been crazy enough to call

Waiting for Old Age

I've decided to embrace old age
give it a big hug
squeeze it tight, break its back
throw it in a mental hole I've dug.

I do not want the ornate cane
or the sturdy metal walker
I'll snap the first in half
and acetylene-torch the other.

I've decided to embrace old age
give it a big hug
squeeze it tight, break its back
teach it not to be so smug.

Maybe I'll hold its hand,
lead it to the oven,
push it in, hike the heat,
so impulsiveness may govern

in the garden of my youth's desires
enabling them to grow
to fan their flames, fuel their fires
to illuminate the last rainbow.

Three Tanka

the absence of you
a shawl across my shoulders
drawn tighter by
the stillness of trees
the silence of birds

watching the moon float
amid cruising charcoal clouds
an ashen buoy
on an onyx ocean
I thought of you tonight

the old dog lies down
headstone shade blankets him
he waits as before
head on the ground dreaming
in smell of earth, scent of home

II.

Early Views

Dedication
for Emily Dickinson

If one poem in this book
scrapes your soul to leave a scar
do not attempt to conceal it
'Tis a beacon to guide me in from afar.

Women are my teachers

Women are my teachers.
They have taught me
how to abuse my body
and condemn my soul.

Men are my gymnasts.
They have shown me
how to contort my mind
and twist my desires.

God is my Keeper.
He has cleaned my cage,
shown His visitors my sores,
and promised twice to free me.

Apostasy

I do not believe
your hands
helped rend a sacrament

On the table your fingers
spread open,
catholic jigsaw puzzle pieces

Your wedding ring's pale shadow
an omen
for the strongest faith

You lay your hands
on mine,
I fall easily from grace

There is no freedom

There is no freedom
in your eyes tonight
You hold your soul
captive
behind frozen brown walls.

There is no freedom
in your voice tonight
You whisper words
conscripted
from restroom graffiti.

There is no freedom
in your hands tonight
You rub lineless palms
misread
by countless gypsy seers.

There is no freedom
for you with me tonight
You keep your chains
locked
with broken pieces of the heart.

Pilgrimage

O love, your body is a song
sung softly in the dark
You keep it from the hobo's humming
as he slumbers peacefully in the park

Your travels are a conspiracy
plotted carefully in your dreams
The twisted lives of men you meet
you straighten out like ancient nylon seams

Your destination is a lie
conceived to deceive us all
The telephone you keep ringing
hangs untouched on a crumbling wall

Your refuge is our farm in Greece
soon to be your favorite pun
I cannot see you burning lonely
beneath a blazing California sun.

It's 3 a.m.

It's 3 a.m.
I've just remembered
what I meant to tell you
but never did.

I forgot to say
the little things
others have already
told you.

I want you to know
I agree.

I have seen your eyes

I have seen your eyes
dance ballets with your words
Dark ballerinas in crystal costumes
they ambush all that is heard

I have watched your smile
betray your looks of sadness
It can commit treason against
any melancholy you possess

I have seen the night sky robbed
of its blackness by your hair
Unseen constellations call you thief
as they hang in colourless air

Having seen the graceful glances
of your eyes, the insurrection
in your smile, and the stolen
midnight of your hair

Ambush me with your eyes
Betray me with your smile
Rob me with your hair

Bouquet of Flowers

This poem is my last
bouquet of flowers
for you.

Mirrors meant
to capture
that which

no flower,
word, world
or man

can ever hope
to trap.

If you read this
late at night,
remember only

certain
jukebox records,
and

soft moments
of conversational touch.

If you read this
in daylight,
remember

words of luck
on summer mornings,
and

smiles of confession
over breakfast.

When I am
no longer
here beside you

read this poem

remember your place
in my life.

Song

Tired
of the Sunday papers

you lay on your back
on the parlor floor

Chestnut hair
fanned out

around beneath and on
your shoulders

a shaman's ritual shawl

Sunlight threads itself
through each soft strand

glistens and winks
a summer's pearl necklace

Unable to speak
too near tears

afternoon shadows
pass your cheek

disappearing
within the silken willows

of your hair
among my indelible

fingerprints and
your mother's witch hazel.

Prelude

You didn't take long
to discover
my weakness

So many others
have tried
and failed

but you were
never like
so many others

Poem

If
you could
only see

the distance
between us

is
the length of
your arms

so motionless
by your body

Lament

Before I left
I meant to trace
the profile of your face
with my finger
brush your curtain hair
with a seashell comb

The way
atavistic artists
prepare portraits
the way
the blind
see to remember

FM 4-6

I have been
on the edge
of this poem

as I charged
windmills of
romantic fantasy,

swung through
jungles on
vines of
feared immaturity,

climbed
tower stairs
to find you
near anonymity,

as you announced
bulletins on some
depressing malady,

wound
wobbling tapes
of a warbling melody,

celebrated
Buffalo Bill's birthday
without cake, candles,
or ceremony.

These words
riot here
demanding

to be heard
while
you are near.

Lady Doctor

I have heard the toy makers
conspiring
to copy your eyes for their dolls
I have stood in the queue to your room
listening
to their plans to put cameras in your walls.

They want to catch your eyes
smiling
as I have often seen them do
They want to patent the tenderness
lying
in them to ensure you cannot sue.

Those who come to you for help
taking
all your prescriptions faithfully
become hypochondriacs
making
each minute with you their remedy.

I stand at your door
seeking
what I should not be looking for
Lady Doctor, you do not have the cure
paralyzing
time and all its moments that we wore.

The vaccine of memory must endure.

Midnight Insanity

I wonder where
you and he will meet?
In Cambridge Square
or down on Marlborough Street?

Will you go again
to one of those places
where you'll assume different names
but keep the same faces?

I hear you give yourself nightly
on a silver spoon
and he only abuses you
under a full autumnal moon.

He'll tire of running
through your many mazes
seeing you through
your phantom psychotic phases.

If he wants to keep you
then I wish him well.
There's room to join
the rest of us in this padded cell.

Dark Shadow

She rises in the early morning hours,
opens the terrace doors in the gloom.
Moonlight masks her garden flowers
gray-green,
ushering dead leaves into her room.

Autumn zephyr whirls round her feet.
She worries it will soon be dawn.
Owl hoots, dog howls, night greets
lost souls
moving in the mist across the lawn.

In shadow where shape shifters thrive,
she is happy, her rapt heart sings.
She hears his whisper as he arrives,
warm death
shrouding her with sated leather wings.

Vampire

Standing
by the unmade bed
watching you dress

he sees
once again
your daily ritual

Stepping
into a skirt
which won't show

too many
of the fingerprints
on your thighs

Pulling
on a turtle-neck sweater
neatly covering

the small
teeth marks
on your neck

Hurrying
into the night,
you throw

a random kiss
and smile
his way

I must remember
not to let you
slip out that door

without telling him
exactly where
you are going.

Hydra 1970

Stone wall stitches
spiral up mountainsides
behind red-roofed rock houses
on which stray tom cats confide.

Chapels on hillsides
closed by time and desertion
cloaked in green moss shawls
relics of the hoary pirates' religion.

Calls of donkeys are its engines
revved up by shrill whistles
from men with wooden whips.
Stone streets are its only trestles.

Above the tourist trap parasites,
where old men with whisk brooms
sweep up donkey dung drowned
in the scent of lilac and poppy fumes,

silent monks kneel down and gaze
upon a gray-hazed Peloponnese
thumbing well-worn worry beads
amid ancient arboreal sentries.

Proteus Revisited

When caught together
in our broken mirror
am I then:

The Ancient Mariner
Quasimodo
Simon at Golgotha

or between
the web of cracks
will I always be:

Porphyria's paramour
Karamazov
Captain Ahab

With my albatross,
humped back,
and wooden cross,

see me as I am:
your desperate, mad,
homicidal lover.

The Last Poem

I wanted you to read this poem last
long after I had gone
so I could slip into your past
leaving only footprints on your lawn.

To A Dying Man On His Birthday

December Seventh

Today is your birthday.
You are twenty-seven
and dying.
You have exactly fifty-five
days to live.

But you have an advantage
most of us
will never have:
you know how
you will die.

You'll be seated
in a chair.
A unique chair.
It will be
a rather simple death.

A switch will be thrown.
Lights will dim.
There will be
only
momentary pain.

A sudden, brain-burning
minute later,
you will be dead.
Toasted,
done over lightly.

The State
will have had
its revenge.
It will say:
"He died to deter others."

And what about the others
who died
to deter you?
Or, don't their deaths count?
If so, not for much.

A hell of a system, isn't it?
You kill. We kill.
And the only one
who really benefits
is the undertaker.

But, don't give up.
Guys have been known
to sit for fifteen years
on the Row,
waiting, just waiting.

But today,
while you sit and wait
for that fifty-fifth day,
I'd just like to say:
Happy Birthday, Richard.

Watching the war

Sitting here
watching the war
in Vietnam

in living
(and dying)
colour

I notice
there are no signs

No signs of protest
are being held up

And if there were
what would they say?
Something like:

TIME TO COME HOME

or

SEND HERSEY BARS

or

MAKE PEACE, NOT LOVE

The more philosophical
might say:

SEND ME AN ARM

or

SEND ME A LEG

or

HELP, I'M A POLITICAL PRISONER

I see none of these

What I do see
are faces
drawn
depressed
disgusted

Eyes
vacant
blood-smeared windows
that have looked out upon
every kind of cruelty and death

Bodies
mud-caked
bug-ridden
bone-tired
hunched-over

bodies of
American men and boys

These must be the signs
they are holding up
for me to see

Arrival in Another City Not for Poets
for Wayne Zade

Stopping my steel horse
in front of my house,
I realize how saddle-sore
how beaten, I am.

The paved whips
of Indiana, Ohio,
New York and
Massachusetts

have left their scars
where only quiet times
and the right woman
can heal them.

Your words of warning
flash
(first red, then green)
in my neon consciousness.

Forgive me, Wayne,
the blind mistress
holding my life's scales
is not feigned.

If I can
I will cheat on her
with metaphor, simile
and random rhyme.

Until meter dulls
the sword she holds,
let this be your new
commemorative stamp.

A Chapter from the Continuing Ballad of Red Ryder

Over milk and coffee brandy,
you tell me you want a wife.
Is this how a free-lance
photographer talks?

What about those
fashion show models,
beauty contest winners
and, ah God yes, losers?

Your 35mm familiar
hangs around your neck
a one-eyed albatross
stuttering only truths.

Checking your exposure speed,
you want to take my picture.
I lick splotches of milk
from my month old moustache.

Down at Billy D's

She's loud and drunk
saying she screws for money
and her old man's in stir
you'd better believe it honey

She lays proud claim
saying she screws for money
Everybody's paid up
you'd better believe it honey

She buys her own
saying she screws for money
But only when in love
you'd better believe it, honey

The Patriots

To the wall
to the wall
our backs
to the wall

At our heads
at our heads
their guns
at our heads

Fingers squeeze
fingers squeeze
palms & triggers
fingers squeeze

In the air
in the air
cries echo
in the air

To the floor
to the floor
bodies fall
to the floor

We are free
we are free
beyond Khartoum
and Wounded Knee

We are free

Summer Haiku

Beaches lying still in the night
beleaguered by beer bottles
branded by salted gray moonlight

It's true

It's true
all the men you knew
wanted you
breathless
with their admiration

left red flowers
ignored on worn doorsteps
purple prose
deleted in unheard voice mail
wasted billboards of adoration

It's true
all the men you knew
wanted you
relentless
with their imagination

All the women

All the women

who have smiled
and combed out
their long hair for me

who have cried
their silent tears
to open their lives for me

they stand
in small rooms
no longer alone

furiously forgetting for me.

III.

At The Next Frontier

The Girl at the Roloi Clock Tower

The girl at the clock tower
speaks all the tongues of man
She smiles and hands the tickets out
to let you in again and again.

You climb the stairs that go on and on
out of breath, wanting to descend
to be with the girl who sells the tickets
and go back to where you once began.

In the Tower at the top
you see the Old and the New
You hear her laugh from far below
It is she, it is you.

Time disguised as Beauty
laughing as you pass
disintegrating into memory
with the sand inside your glass.

Hydra 2006

Ancient
streets without cars
wind between white rock houses
on hillsides stitched with stone walls
crumbling

where bright
red poppies grow
wild among the tall pines
while silent monastic monks pray
all night

til dawn
when church bells ring
through the horseshoe harbor
where old men with donkeys sweep up
the dung

and wait
for the tourists
from ferries and long yachts
to pay for rides and marvel at
the view.

Women and their crimes

I met my Lady weeping
She said "I've wronged a man"
I let her cry upon my shoulder
She stopped and took my hand.

I gave my Lady a poem
She said "I want a song"
I put my words to music
She said it was too long.

I gave my Lady a flower
She said "I want a garden"
I planted seed, when it bloomed
She granted me a pardon.

I gave my Lady comfort
She said "I want more"
I held her a moment longer
She smiled and closed the door.

I sent my Lady messages
She never answered back
I've tried so hard to reach her
She's taken silence as her tack.

The moral of this story
The moral of these lines
is not to feel too sorry
for women and their crimes.

Godin and Ovation

Godin and Ovation
will be my orphans
Alone, when I am gone
silent, waiting
their cases the same
as my casket

who will resurrect *them*

dust
their smooth frets
wax
their handsome bodies
caress
their caring strings

allowing them
to sing again

until music itself ceases

Crazy

with an apology to H.D. Thoreau

Crazy is the detergent
scrubbing the scum
of quiet desperation
from the wheels of destiny.

Crazy is the roulette ball
coming to rest
on your odd number
when all your friends are even.

Crazy is the last chance
to forego the normalcy
no one can define
but everyone claims to have

and to dance
naked and alone
on ancient marble stairs
unafraid of history,

yours or theirs,
as cold stone numbs
blisters burning
the soles of your gypsy feet.

Don Quixote after therapy

I'm broken and I'm bitter
by the heart's forced retreat
the fundamental loss
incurred with aged love's defeat

I knelt whenever beauty passed
laid down my heavy lance
arose a better man each time
encouraged by her glance

I fought and died for beauty
not knowing I was unarmed
she never promised anything
never said I'd go unharmed

I'm bitter and I'm broken
by aged love's defeat
the fundamental loss
incurred with the heart's forced retreat

I don't recognize that image
in the hallway mirror
the grey and wrinkled flesh
inside this phony armor

the glacial cold of loneliness
freezes me on crowded streets
where deformed and crippled hearts
still pause yet never care to meet

they've taken down the road signs
that marked the narrow ways
I wandered for a lifetime
within this twisted maze

I'm broken and I'm bitter
by the heart's forced retreat
the fundamental loss
incurred with aged love's defeat

Identity

I wanted
to be known
as a man
with amazing art

to be seen
as a man
with an incendiary heart

But I came
to be known
as a man
who just plays his part

to be seen
as a man
with an asbestos heart

It's not drawn
that way at all
you know
that yellow tattered chart

to be found
among the ashes
of my inflammable heart.

Broken Borders

I've broken all the borders hindering my advance
Scouting old horizons from a torn and yellowed chart
Listening to the music, relearning how to dance

Outside the known casinos, risking my last chance
Sculpting new contours within the landscape of the heart
I've broken all the borders hindering my advance

Left the faithful and familiar without a backward glance
As others have before me within their lonely art
Listening to the music, relearning how to dance

To songs on the radio with lost lyrics of romance
And my pockets full of essays excoriating Sartre
I've broken all the borders hindering my advance

Dreams derived from written words spoken to enhance
Tepid transit letters kept clandestine by Bogart
Listening to the music, relearning how to dance

With time a metered measure, the dancers take a stance
Hope draws Redemption closer, as the last song starts
I've broken all the borders hindering my advance
Listening to the music, relearning how to dance

Acknowledgements

I am grateful to the editors of the following literary journals where some of these poems first appeared:

"Evangelismos" and "Night in Rhodes" first appeared in *Concise Delight,* Summer 2009
"Hydra 2006" first appeared as "Idra 2006" in the Spring 2008 volume of *Shadow Quill Poetry*
"Identity" first appeared in *Popt Art*, Spring 2011
"On the First Anniversary of the Night the Red Sox Won the World Series (October 25, 2005)" first appeared in *The Write Action No. 2 Tenth Anniversary Anthology* (2011)
"To a Dying Man on His Birthday" first appeared in a small mimeographed literary magazine (name now forgotten) in California in 1968.
"Three Tanka" first appeared in *Modern English Tanka*, Volume 2, Number 2 (Winter 2007)

I will be forever grateful to John Matthias, professor emeritus at the University of Notre Dame. I went to his classes to learn about the important poets of our time and with a desire to write poetry. I came out of those classes with the realization that I had been taught by one of those very poets who had turned my desire to write into a *need* to write, a life gift of immeasurable value.

I also want to thank my fellow writers who always encourage and inspire me in my work, especially Leo Beaudet and Laura Havens.

Thanks as well to those who offer not only encouragement and inspiration but also support, not least among them, my wife Robin, my daughter Alissa, and my son Justin. Thank you for your understanding of this addiction and, most importantly, for just being there.

About the Author

John L. Holgerson's poetry has appeared in literary journals such as *Modern English Tanka, Shadow Quill Poetry, Popt Art, Concise Delight,* and *The Write Action No. 2 Tenth Anniversary Anthology.* He holds a Bachelor of Arts and Juris Doctor from the University of Notre Dame where he studied under the American poet, John Matthias, now professor emeritus and co-editor of the Notre Dame Review. For three decades, he was a trial and appellate attorney for the Massachusetts Defenders Committee and for its later incarnation as the Public Counsel Division of the Committee for Public Counsel Services. He now practices law in a small firm in Taunton, Massachusetts and is at work on his first novel. *Broken Borders* is his first collection of poetry.

CPSIA information can be obtained at www.ICGtesting.com
Printed in the USA
BVOW071104030212

282102BV00001B/2/P

Praise for **The Thief**

"*The Thief* brings to mind Highsmith, Mishima and Doestoevsky . . . A chilling existential thriller leaving readers in doubt without making them feel in any way cheated."
—*Wall Street Journal*, Best Book of the Year Selection

"I was deeply impressed with *The Thief*. It is fresh. It is sure to enjoy a great deal of attention." —Kenzaburō Ōe, Nobel Prize-winning author of *A Personal Matter*

"Fascinating. I want to write something like *The Thief* someday myself."
—Natsuo Kirino, bestselling author of Edgar-nominated *Out* and *Grotesque*

"An intelligent, compelling and surprisingly moving tale, and highly recommended." —*The Guardian*

"Nakamura's prose is cut-to-the-bone lean, but it moves across the page with a seductive, even voluptuous agility. I defy you not to finish the book in a single sitting." —*Richmond Times-Dispatch*

"Fuminori Nakamura's Tokyo is not a city of bright lights, bleeding-edge technology, and harajuku girls with bubblegum pink hair. In Nakamura's Japan, the lights are broken, the knives are bloodier than the tech, and the harajuku girls are aging single mothers turning tricks in cheap tracksuits. His grasp of the seamy underbelly of the city is why Nakamura is one of the most award-winning young guns of Japanese hardboiled detective writing." —*Daily Beast*

"It's simple and utterly compelling—a great beach reading for the deeply cynical. What you'd get if you crossed Michael Connelly and Camus and translated it from Japanese." —*Grantland*

"Surreal." —*Sacramento Bee*, "Page-Turner" Pick

"Nakamura's writing is spare, taut, with riveting descriptions . . . Nakamura conjures dread, and considers philosophical questions of fate and control . . . For all the thief's anonymity, we come to know his skill, his powerlessness and his reach for life."

—*Cleveland Plain Dealer*

"Nakamura's memorable antihero, at once as believably efficient as Donald Westlake's Parker and as disaffected as a Camus protagonist, will impress genre and literary readers alike."   —*Publishers Weekly*

"Compulsively readable for its portrait of a dark, crumbling, graffiti-scarred Tokyo—and the desire to understand the mysterious thief."

—*Booklist*

"Disguised as fast-paced, shock-fueled crime fiction, *The Thief* resonates even more as a treatise on contemporary disconnect and paralyzing isolation."   —*Library Journal*

"Nakamura's dark imagination gives rise to his literary world . . . the influences of Kafka and Dostoyevsky are not hard to spot.

—*The Japan Times*

"Fast-paced, elegantly written, and rife with the symbols of inevitability."

—*ForeWord*

"*The Thief* manages to wrap you up in its pages, tightly, before you are quite aware of it."   —*Mystery Scene*

"[An] extremely well-written tale . . . Readers will be enthralled by this story that offers an extremely surprising ending."—*Suspense Magazine*

"Nakamura succeeds in creating a complicated crime novel in which the focus is not on the crimes themselves but rather on the psychology and physicality of the criminal. The book's power inheres in the voice of the thief, which is itself as meticulously rendered as the thief's every action."   —*Three Percent*

"Both a crime thriller and a character study, it is a unique and engrossing read, keeping a distant yet thoughtful eye on the people it follows . . . It's a haunting undercurrent, making *The Thief* a book that's hard to shake once you've read it."   —*Mystery People*

"The drily philosophical tone and the noir atmosphere combine perfectly, providing a rapid and enjoyable 'read' that is nonetheless cool and distant, provoking the reader to think about (as much as experience) the tale."   —International Noir Fiction

The Thief

Also by Fuminori Nakamura

The
Thief

FUMINORI NAKAMURA

Translated from the Japanese by

SATOKO IZUMO and STEPHEN COATES

SOHO

First published in English in 2012 by
Soho Press
853 Broadway
New York, NY 10003

Library of Congress Cataloging-in-Publication Data

Nakamura, Fuminori, 1977–
[Suri. English]
The thief / Fuminori Nakamura.

ISBN 978-1-61695-202-0
eISBN 978-1-61695-022-4
1. Thieves—Japan—Fiction. 2. Tokyo (Japan)—Fiction. I. Title.
PL873.5.A339S8713 2012
895.6'36—dc23
2011041972

Printed in the United States of America

10 9 8 7 6 5 4

The Thief

1 When I was a kid, I often messed this up.

In crowded shops, in other people's houses, things I'd pick up furtively would slip from my fingers. Strangers' possessions were like foreign objects that didn't fit comfortably in my hands. They would tremble faintly, asserting their independence, and before I knew it they'd come alive and fall to the ground. The point of contact, which was intrinsically morally wrong, seemed to be rejecting me. And in the distance there was always the tower. Just a silhouette floating in the mist like some ancient daydream. But I don't make mistakes like that these days. And naturally I don't see the tower either.

IN FRONT OF me a man in his early sixties was walking towards the platform, in a black coat with a silver suitcase in his right hand. Of all the passengers here, I was sure he was the richest. His coat was Brunello Cucinelli, and so was his suit. His Berluti shoes, probably made to order, did not show even the slightest scuff marks. His wealth was obvious to everyone around him. The silver watch peeping out from the cuff on his left wrist was a Rolex Datejust. Since he wasn't used to taking the bullet train by himself, he was having some trouble buying a ticket. He stooped forward, his thick fingers hovering over the vending machine uncertainly like revolting caterpillars. At that moment I saw his wallet in the left front pocket of his jacket.

Keeping my distance, I got on the escalator, got off at a leisurely pace. With a newspaper in my hand, I stood behind him as he waited for the train. My heart was beating a little fast. I knew the position of all the security cameras on this platform. Since I only had a platform ticket, I had to finish the job before he boarded the train. Blocking the view of the people to my right with my back, I folded the paper as I switched it to my left hand. Then I lowered it slowly to create a shield and slipped my right index and middle fingers into his coat pocket. The fluorescent light glinted faintly off the button on his cuff, sliding at the edge of my vision. I breathed in gently and held it, pinched the corner of the wallet and pulled it out. A quiver ran from my fingertips to my shoulder and a warm sensation gradually spread throughout my body. I felt like I was standing in a void, as though with the countless intersecting lines of vision of all those people, not one was directed at me. Maintaining the fragile contact between my fingers and the wallet, I sandwiched it in the folded newspaper. Then I transferred the paper to my right hand and put it in the inside pocket of my own coat. Little by little I breathed out, conscious of my temperature rising even more. I checked my surroundings, only my eyes moving. My fingers still held the tension of touching a forbidden object, the numbness of entering someone's personal space. A trickle of sweat ran down my back. I took out my cell phone and pretended to check my email as I walked away.

I went back to the ticket gate and down the gray stairs towards the Marunouchi line. Suddenly one of my eyes blurred, and all the people moving around me seemed to shimmer, their silhouettes distorted. When I reached the platform I spotted a man in a black suit out of the corner of my eye. I located his wallet by the slight bulge in the right back pocket of his trousers. From his appearance and demeanor I judged him to be a successful male companion at a ladies-only club. He was looking quizzically at his phone, his slender fingers moving busily over the keys. I got on the train with him, reading the flow of the crowd, and positioned myself behind him in the muggy carriage. When humans' nerves detect big and small stimuli at the same time, they ignore the smaller one. On this section of track there are two large curves where the train shakes violently. The office worker behind me was reading an evening paper, folded up small, and the two middle-aged women on my right were gossiping about someone and laughing raucously. The only one who wasn't simply traveling was me. I turned the back of my hand towards the man and took hold of his wallet with two fingers. The other passengers formed a wall around me on two sides. Two threads at the corner of his pocket were frayed and twisted, forming elegant spirals like snakes. As the train swayed I pushed my chest close to him as though leaning against his back and then pulled the wallet out verti-cally. The tight pressure inside me leaked into the air. I breathed out and a reassuring warmth flowed through my body. Without moving I checked the atmosphere in the carriage, but nothing seemed out of order. There was no way I would make a mistake in a simple job like this. At the next station I got off and walked away, hunching my shoulders like someone feeling the cold.

I joined the stream of weary people and went through the barrier. Looking at the fifteen or so average men and women gathered at the entrance to the station, I figured there was about two hundred thousand yen among them. I strolled off, lighting a cigarette. Behind a power pole to my left I saw a man check the contents of his wallet in full view and put it in the right pocket of his white down jacket. His cuffs were dark with stains, his sneakers worn and only the fabric of his jeans was good quality. I ignored him and went into Mitsukoshi Department Store. On the menswear floor, which was full of brand-name shops, there was a display mannequin wearing a coordinated outfit, something reasonably well-off guys in their late twenties or early thirties would wear. The mannequin and I were dressed the same. I had no interest in clothes, but people in my line of work can't afford to stand out. You have to look prosperous so that no one suspects you. You have to wear a lie, you have to blend into your environment as a lie. The only difference between me and the store dummy was the shoes. Keeping in mind that I might have to run away, I was in sneakers.

I took advantage of the warmth inside the shop to loosen my fingers, opening and closing my hands inside my pockets. The wet handkerchief I used to moisten my fingers was still cold. My forefinger and middle finger were almost the same length. Whether I was born like that or they gradually grew that way I don't know. People whose ring fingers are longer than their index fingers use their middle and ring fingers. Some people grip with three fingers, with the middle finger at the back. Like all forms of motion, there is a smooth, ideal movement for removing a wallet from a pocket. It's not only a matter of the angle, but of speed as well. Ishiwaka loved talking about this stuff. Often when he drank he became unguarded and chatty like a child. I didn't know what he was up to anymore. I figured he was probably already dead.

I entered a stall in the department store's dimly lit toilet, pulled on a thin pair of gloves and inspected the wallets. I'd made it a rule never to use the station toilets, just to be on the safe side. The Brunello Cucinelli man's held 96,000 yen, three American $100 bills, a Visa gold card, an American Express gold card, a driver's license, a gym membership card and a receipt for 72,000 yen from a fancy Japanese restaurant. Just when I was about to give up I found an intricately colored plastic card with nothing printed on it. I'd come across these before. They're for exclusive private brothels. In the male companion's wallet were 52,000 yen, a driver's license, a Mitsui Sumitomo credit card, cards for Tsutaya video store and a comic book café, several business cards from sex workers and a whole lot of scrap paper, receipts and the like. There were also some colorful pills with hearts and stars stamped on them. I only took the banknotes, leaving the rest inside. A wallet shows a person's personality and lifestyle. Just like a cell phone, it is at the center, forming the nucleus of the owner's secrets, everything he carries on him. I never sold the cards because it was too much bother. I did what Ishikawa would have done—if I dropped the wallets in a mailbox, the post office would forward them to the police, who would then return them to the address on the driver's license. I wiped off my fingerprints and put the wallets in my pocket. The male escort might get busted for drugs, but that wasn't my problem.

Just as I was leaving the stall I felt something strange in one of the hidden pockets inside my coat. Alarmed, I went back into the toilet. A Bulgari wallet, made of stiff leather. Inside was 200,000 yen in new bills. Also several gold cards, Visa and others, and the business cards of the president of a securities firm. I'd never seen the wallet or the name on the cards before.

Not again, I thought. I had no recollection of taking it. But of all the wallets I'd acquired that day it was definitely the most valuable.

2

Feeling a slight headache, I gave myself up to the rocking of the train. It was bound for Haneda Airport, but it was terribly crowded. Between the heating and the warmth of other people's bodies, I was sweating. I stared out the window, moving my fingers in my pockets. Clusters of dingy houses passed at regular intervals, like some kind of code. Suddenly I remembered the last wallet I took yesterday. I blinked and an enormous iron tower flashed by me with a loud roar. It was over in an instant but my body stiffened. The tower was tall and I felt like it had glanced casually at me standing tensely in the middle of that crowded train.

When I looked around the carriage I saw a man who seemed to be totally absorbed by something. Not so much concentrating as in a trance, eyes half closed, as he groped a woman's body. I think that men like that fall into two types—ordinary people who have perverted tendencies, and people who are swallowed up by their perversion so that the boundary between fantasy and reality becomes blurred and then disappears completely. I suspected he belonged to the second group. Then I realized that the victim was a junior high school student, and I wove my way through a gap in the crowd. Apart from me and him and the girl, no one had noticed anything.

From behind, I deliberately grabbed the man's left wrist with my left hand. All his muscles suddenly jerked into life and then I felt him go limp, as though after a severe shock. Keeping hold of his wrist, I steadied his watch with my forefinger, undid the clasp on the strap with my thumb and slid it into my sleeve. Then I pinched his wallet from the right inside pocket of his suit with my right fingers. Realizing there was a risk of touching his body, I changed my movement, dropped the wallet in the space between his jacket and shirt and caught it with my left hand underneath. A company employee in his late thirties, and judging from his ring he was married. I grasped his arm again, this time with my right hand. The color had drained from his face and he was struggling to turn towards me, twisting his neck while rocking with the motion of the train. Sensing the change behind her, the girl moved her head, unsure whether to turn around or not. The carriage was quiet. The man was trying to open his mouth to speak, as if he wanted to justify himself to me or to the world. It seemed like some malevolent spotlight was calling attention to his presence. His throat quivered as though he was getting ready to scream. Sweat was running down his cheeks and forehead and his eyes were wide but unfocused. Perhaps I would wear the same expression when I got caught. I released the pressure on his arm and mouthed, "Go!" Face contorted, he couldn't make up his mind. I jerked my head towards the door. Arms trembling, he turned to the front again, as if he'd realized that I'd been looking at his face. The door opened and he ran. He thrust his way into the throng, wriggling and shoving people out of the way.

Inside the carriage the schoolgirl was staring at me. I turned away, trying to suppress my revulsion. I'd taken a watch I didn't want, a wallet I didn't want, and both the man and the girl had seen what I looked like. At least there was no way he could report me.

My heart was no longer in it so I got off at the next stop. On the escalator I spotted the slack, wealthy face of a middle-aged man, but I went outside and rested against the dirty wall. The tension was gradually leaving my body. I warmed my fingers in my pockets, thinking about catching a taxi.

I felt someone's presence and when I looked around a skinny guy was just leaning on the wall beside me. A black suit, a brand I didn't recognize, black shoes I didn't recognize. *It's Tachibana*, I thought. Caught off guard, I started to panic and fought to control myself. His hair, which had been blond, was now dyed brown. Staring fixedly at me through narrowed eyes, he curled his thick lips. It might have been a smile, but I wasn't sure.

"I thought you only targeted rich people?"

As he said this he turned his whole body to face me. Tachibana might not have been his real name, but I was pretty sure he knew mine. I thought I'd meet him somewhere, but I expected that when I did I'd be the one to spot him. All my memories came flooding back and I took a deep breath.

"Yeah, I do."

I wanted to say something else, but this inane reply was all I could come up with.

"That's boring. Besides, do really rich people ride trains? You're a crook, so act like one."

"I just go with the flow. So, you're still alive."

"I'm talking to you, aren't I? I've been watching you."

"Since when?"

"The whole time. Since you took that pervert's wallet. I'm a bit surprised you didn't realize I was following you."

I started to walk and he walked with me. We went under the railway bridge and I stopped.

"How long have you been here?" he asked.

For some reason he was looking at me seriously.

"Not long. After all, there's easy pickings in Tokyo. This and that."

"But it must be hard on your own. I'm free. Why don't we team up?"

"I'm fine. I don't trust your skills and I don't trust you to share either."

He laughed loudly and started walking again. Deliberately loud laughter makes people uncomfortable, and although Tachibana must have known that he didn't stop. When we came out on the other side of the railway bridge I felt as though the massive structures, the department stores and buildings, were glaring down at me from behind. A shiver ran down my spine and I found myself staring at the wilted grass poking up through the concrete. Tachibana stopped, leaned against a wire mesh fence and lit a cigarette.

"Sure, I'm not that good. I was originally a shoplifter, back in junior high school. Picking pockets was just an extension of that, just for fun. I can't do it like you or Ishikawa. You doing the lift, passing the wallet to him, he takes out what's inside and then you put it back in the owner's pocket. And then he'd only take two thirds. The mark wouldn't realize what had happened, and even if he did he couldn't report it. And the way you guys shared the roles, changing positions and taking turns. Signaling just with your eyes. All I could do was watch in awe. But there are hardly any Japanese pickpockets these days. Are you still changing jobs all the time? If you need a sideline, why not join another pro burglary ring, like you did before, or deal, or something? Has pickpocketing turned into your main job? "

Because of the nature of our conversation I had to move closer to him.

"I used to sell fakes. What's good now?"

"Loan-sharking's gone out of fashion, and I was using some young guys for bank transfer scams. Now it's stocks. Of course, I'm just a go-between."

"Stocks?"

"I'm not a nobody any more. The yakuza give me money, which I pass on to someone else to invest. Their information is amazing. Insider trading, that's what I'm talking about. Everyone's doing it these days."

He tossed away his cigarette butt.

"I'm making heaps more than you. I could put some work your way. All you'd have to do is just give some filthy rooms to a bunch of homeless people. In return, you get them to set up bank accounts, which we can use for a whole range of scams without there being any connection to us."

"I'm not interested."

"You're weird. So was Ishikawa. What is it you want?"

I stayed silent.

"Well, aren't you going to ask what happened to him?"

He was watching me. My heart started to beat faster.

"Do you know?"

"No," he said and laughed.

The sunlight overhead was really bothering me.

"But it had something to do with that robbery, I guess. One thing's for sure. That was spooky. It's spooky when a big job like that goes off without a hitch. I bet he got into trouble then. I'll tell you one thing, though. You should get out of Tokyo, especially this area."

"Why?"

"It looks like they're up to something again."

Our eyes met. I wasn't sure how to respond, so I looked at the ground.

"You should disappear, before you get caught up in it again."

"What about you?"

"I'll be OK. In fact, if they are planning something I'll make a lot of cash. Besides, that's how I live. It's too late to worry about saving my own skin."

He laughed, so I laughed too. As if realizing that he'd talked for too long, he raised his hand lightly and turned at the intersection. In the distance I saw a tall, rich-looking man, but I couldn't be bothered. The buildings were getting to me, so I went back under the bridge. Murky water had pooled in a discarded take-out container. Somehow it looked unpleasantly warm.

3 I was lying on my bed unable to sleep. I opened my eyes. The rain was buffeting the thin windows, making an unpleasant rattling noise. A deep bass beat pounded from the apartment above. From time to time it stopped, then started again, over and over. I was wide awake, fully aware of every detail of my ground-floor room. The rain seemed inexorable, falling from the sky to inundate the whole world around me.

The pulsing rhythm overhead stopped, leaving just the sound of the rain. When the music didn't start again, I figured the guy upstairs had gone to sleep. I felt like I was the only person left in the whole world. I lit a cigarette, then saw that there was a half-finished one still in the ashtray. My room held nothing worth looking at, just a pipe bed and a closet and an ironing board. Synthetic fibers stuck up like stakes from the holes in the frayed tatami mats. I stared at my long fingers, flexing them over and over, opening, closing. I tried to remember when I first realized that I was virtually ambidextrous, but couldn't pin it down. It felt like I'd been born with it, but also like I gradually grew that way.

The rain kept on falling as if it was determined not to let me go outside. I contemplated the vastness of the clouds in the sky, and the place I was in at that moment. Like an act of defiance, I grabbed my cigarettes, pulled on my socks, opened the flimsy wooden door and stepped outside. The rain soaked the rusty poles of the apartment building, the bicycle lying on its side like a corpse, making the cold air even colder.

I rounded the corner by a leaning traffic sign, walked past a factory with rusting steps, then turned left at the

T-junction at the end of a line of row houses. A car was coming towards me, picking up speed. I guessed that it would give way first and sure enough, when I feinted towards it, it swerved timidly. Many telephone poles away the rain was lashing a gigantic pylon. I looked away, but of course I knew it was there even if I wasn't watching it.

When I got to the station the downpour was drenching a solitary taxi with no passengers. The driver was looking straight ahead listlessly, eyes still, staring into space. I climbed the stairs and closed my umbrella. A homeless man, lying there out of the rain and cold, was looking in my direction. He seemed right at home, as though there was supposed to be a bum here at this hour. Something about his eyes reminded me of Ishikawa and I felt uneasy, but his face and age were wrong. He wasn't actually looking at me. He was gazing fixedly at a point just behind me as I walked, as if there was something there. I lit a smoke to take my mind off him, crossed over to the other side of the tracks and down the dilapidated steps.

In a convenience store I bought some more cigarettes and a can of coffee. When I handed over the money the clerk bellowed, "Thank you very much!" like he was insane. The cash was what I'd taken from the pervert the day before, but its previous owners were unknown. I thought about how this banknote had witnessed a moment of each one of those people's lives. Maybe it had been at the scene of a murder, then passed from the murderer to a shopkeeper somewhere, then to a good person somewhere else.

When I left the store the great, fat clouds seemed to be hovering overhead, and I felt like I was being coated with countless drops of rain. My heart started to beat faster and I flexed my fingers in my pockets. I imagined calling a cab, getting out in some busy area and sliding my fingers into the people's pockets there—planting myself in the middle of the crowd, one wallet after another, my hands moving as swiftly and precisely as possible. The rain kept falling and my pulse wouldn't settle. I thought the only thing for it was to go downtown, but I tried to compose myself. I climbed the stairs once more, telling myself that the persistent footsteps behind me were just echoes, and lit another cigarette. The homeless man was nowhere to be seen. My heart beating dully, heavily, I went through the station and downstairs again. A man in a raincoat was getting saturated at the roundabout in front of me and the white headlights of a passing car lit up the drizzle, illuminating the sharp, golden droplets. The rain seemed to hold a thousand needles. I spotted the sleeping figure of the homeless guy but there was no sign of the man in the raincoat.

I stopped myself from looking over my shoulder, thinking that I shouldn't have come out in the first place. I could sense the pylon, even though I couldn't see it from here. I felt the never-ending rain. I was conscious of the enormous clouds and of myself walking beneath them.

4 "If you steal a hundred thousand from someone who's worth a billion, it's almost like you've taken nothing."

Ishikawa often used to say things like that. He loved stealing from the rich, and I would just go along with it. He'd take their wallets, but he didn't really care about the money and spent most of it immediately.

"But it's still wrong," I said.

He nodded, but he grinned briefly before continuing the conversation. We were chatting in a narrow booth in our usual run-down bar. The owner was a former gangster, though he never said much about his past. His arms and legs were thin and his body twisted, giving him a slightly lopsided appearance. I couldn't tell his age.

"But obviously if there was no concept of ownership there'd be no concept of stealing, would there? As long as there's one starving child in the world, all property is theft."

"We can't use that to excuse what we do, though."

"I'm not trying to excuse it. I just can't stand people who are totally convinced that they're saints."

Ishikawa once stole a lot of money with a really simple trick. He heard about this old man who used to go to a private club with a large bundle of cash. The man was the director of some religious organization and he liked showing off his money to young women. After every assembly, to work off some of his exaltation, he'd take his staff to this club to have sex with the girls there. He was scrawny and bug-eyed, with a habit of showing his gums when he laughed. Ishikawa bought a pouch exactly the same as the one the old guy carried his cash in, waited for him to turn up at the club, and as they were getting out of the car he bumped into the secretary who was carrying the bag. He shoved the pouch inside his coat and dropped the fake one, which was stuffed with wads of paper. The old man picked it up, barking at an apologetic Ishikawa before disappearing into the grey building with his assistants. The bag contained ten million yen.

"I guess he likes round numbers like ten million. No, he isn't a bad person at heart. Probably he really did want to build schools in the Sudan and help refugees and stuff, just like they advertise. Subconsciously. So I helped him realize his subconscious desire."

Ishikawa screwed up his face and laughed like a child.

"Look, in those countries there are thousands of people who die as soon as they're born, right? Just because they were unlucky enough to be born in that place, Dying in droves with no time to fight back, all skin and bone and covered in flies. I'd hate that."

I don't know if it's true or not, but he said that he gave one million yen to his accomplice, a woman from some foreign country who worked in the club. Then he spent another million the same day and sent the rest to an overseas non-profit where his ex-girlfriend worked.

Ishikawa was always good with his hands and he had a smooth tongue. In the past he'd drifted from one job to the next, only picking pockets when he needed money. Before I met him he was in a notorious investment fraud group.

"When I'm making my way invisibly through a crowd, it's a special feeling. You know how time has different textures? The tension when you're gambling or pulling off some investment scam is the same. The instant you move outside the law or sleep with some woman who's off limits, like a mobster's girlfriend, time becomes saturated. It's ecstasy. Intense moments like those demand to be recreated, taking on a personality of their own. They tell you, again, I want that feeling again. Well, for me picking pockets is the greatest thrill of all."

An arrest warrant was issued for Ishikawa for fraud and he fled to the Philippines, and then as far as Pakistan and Kenya. When he came back, however, he'd acquired a dead person's identity. He had a new driver's license and passport and certificate of residence—on the face of it he was a free man.

"The official story is that I died in Pakistan, so now my name's Niimi. That means I was already Niimi when I met you. It's complicated and I can't go into details, but there are some things you're better off not knowing."

Because of the demands of the part of his life I wasn't supposed to ask about, he spent Monday to Friday in an office all by himself, watching the phone. From time to time a call would come in and he'd answer with the name of a company that was probably fictitious. He collected the mail and very occasionally he'd receive a visit from a man who appeared to be some sort of official. Going out on the town with me was pretty much limited to Saturdays and Sundays.

At his request I went to the office several times to keep him company. But as fate would have it, when I was there one day I met the man. The door flew open, I spun round in surprise and there he was, right in front of me. At the entrance he turned off the light and looked silently around the room. I don't know why, but the moment I saw him I regretted having come. In the darkness, without saying a word, the man walked inside.

With his black hair and sunglasses he looked like a broker of some kind, but I couldn't guess his age. He could have been thirty, he could have been fifty. In the dim light shining though the curtain his shadow stretched along the wall. Naturally it moved when he moved, and his footsteps rang out strangely. Still watching Ishikawa, he opened the safe, took out ten million yen or so and stuffed it casually into a bag. Then he turned his attention to me for some reason.

"I'll see you again," he muttered.

I had no idea what was going on so I just stared back at him. After the man left, however, Ishikawa went on talking about pickpocketing, as if he didn't want to give me a chance to open my mouth.

"There's only been one time I really didn't like dipping. It was a fireworks display, see? It's pretty unusual, but sometimes you get some rich people mingling with the crowd, right?"

Looking at his face I gave up on asking about the man. Probably he fell into that category of things I was better off not knowing about. I tried to forget about him, though not very successfully.

"A middle-aged guy watching from his hotel room with his mistress, for example. She starts pestering him to go down and get yakisoba, or wants to go for a walk together or something. Ever since I was a kid I've loved fireworks. Poor people can see them for free and they're great entertainment. Up in the sky, they're equally nice for everyone."

Sometimes Ishikawa's expression was so innocent that he looked defenseless, but the echoes of the man still lingered in the room, and his eyes wouldn't stay still.

"They're really beautiful. One of the most beautiful things in this life, in the world. But we take advantage of that beauty, yeah? We're waiting for a chance, when everyone's absorbed in the beauty. We're not looking at the fireworks, we're looking at people's pockets. That's—I don't know how to describe it."

That's what he said, but for me it was his skill that was enchanting. Nipping a wallet with three fingers, passing it back to me, and by the time I took out the money and return it he'd already have lifted the next one. Then he would lean his arm against the first wallet's owner and without even looking he would put it back in the guy's pocket again. In my eyes his movements were one of life's beauties. At the time it never occurred to me that this beauty would vanish as swiftly as the fireworks.

5 When I went outside again the rain had stopped, so I dumped my umbrella in the basket of a nearby bike. I buttoned my coat, ignoring the cat that had been following me for some reason, and went into a supermarket.

It was warm in the shop and I started to sweat. I thought I spotted Tachibana, but then realized there was no reason for him to be there and exhaled in relief. One of the staff was watching me. I put bread, ham and eggs into my basket, grabbed a bottle of mineral water and headed for the checkout.

I was trying to work out why I'd come back to Tokyo. Ever since that violent, elaborately planned attack, I'd known it was dangerous to return. I wanted news of Ishikawa, but I wasn't sure if that was the real reason. Thinking about how the situation had unfolded back then, I knew there was a strong possibility that he was dead, and almost certainly it wasn't safe for me to be here either.

I noticed a mother with her child and I stopped. The woman, her damaged hair tied in a ponytail, touched the boy lightly with her knee. At that moment he slipped a packet of fish fillets into the Uniqlo bag he was carrying. A towel had been placed inside and by shaking the paper bag the stuff was hidden. My heart skipped a beat and I was annoyed with myself. The child was seizing the items earnestly, as though trying to live up to his mother's expectations. He was skillful, and he seemed determined that even if he were caught his mother wouldn't be blamed. Skinny legs poked out from his blue shorts and the sleeves and pockets of his green jacket were frayed.

Inside the shop, with its cheerful piped music, they were conspicuous. I stood and looked at the boy's clothes. The woman smacked him, maybe because he was walking too slowly. People turned to stare, but he was smiling. I thought he was probably ashamed. His smile looked automatic, insisting to the onlookers that he wasn't the kind of kid who gets treated like that by his mother and that his mother wasn't that sort of parent, trying to mask his mother's disgrace.

I found myself following them. She nudged the boy with her knee again and he swiftly put some cup noodles in the bag. His hands were quick, but the bag was too small to meet his mother's demands. A middle-aged woman in a dark blue coat disappeared around the corner of the aisle, keeping an eye on them. I was certain she was a store detective, employed by the supermarket to catch shoplifters. The child seemed to have noticed, but he couldn't tell his mother.

I approached them and examined the woman from up close. She was in her mid-thirties, with narrow eyes and a haggard look. Her red tracksuit was new but her sandals were ugly and dirty. She crouched down to inspect the biscuits, prodding them with her finger and mumbling to herself as if unable to make up her mind. I suddenly thought of Saeko, even though this woman didn't look a bit like her. When she reached out for a packet of crackers and turned to call her son, I was squatting beside her. I realized that I was about to say something so I stopped myself and started to rise, but she was looking at me in surprise. Seeing her face, I felt as though the words were dragged out of me.

"You've been busted."

"What?"

She glared at me, disguising her fear with anger. The boy stood petrified beside her, skinny and miserable.

"The woman in the navy coat over there. She works for the store. You've definitely been spotted. These days they call the cops straight away, so either buy it or dump it all and leave."

The mother's desires had greatly exceeded the capacity of the towel in the clumsily modified paper bag the child was carrying. The meat and fish were hidden, but I could see the tip of a bulging packet of snacks. I went to the checkout and joined a queue. It was busy.

People were jammed together like ants and everyone was sweating.

After I left the shop I bought a can of coffee, which I'd forgotten to get inside, from a vending machine. I lit a cigarette as the woman and child came walking up behind me. The boy undid the lock on his mother's bike and watched her back as she approached me.

"Who the hell are you?"

For an instant her face contorted, one eye closing, squeezed tight at the edge. As she stood in front of me the tic showed itself again.

"All I did was warn you that you'd been seen."

"Are you laughing at me?"

She glared at me and her eye shut firmly yet again.

"I'm feeding my kid properly. It's not fair to laugh at me."

Behind her the boy seemed to be assessing how angry she was. Her voice was unnaturally loud, as though her wiring was faulty somewhere, and as I looked at her face I thought once more of Saeko.

"Sometimes I feel happy when people tell me I've done something unforgivable," Saeko once said to me. "Even when I didn't do it on purpose. Because I do nasty things to everyone. Because I do nasty things to myself as well. Because I trample all over people's values."

Saeko's voice was always low.

"I'm not laughing at you," I said to the woman.

I took out the coffee I'd just bought.

"Because I've shoplifted too. I only told you because you'd been seen. You should be grateful."

The woman had opened her eyes and was sizing me up. I didn't think Saeko had ever looked at me with that expression.

"Who are you?"

"Doesn't matter."

"Where do you work?"

"I don't."

I was telling the truth, but she was looking me up and down. I was wearing my good clothes, as I always did when I went into the city at night.

"But you've got money, haven't you? Give me a call when you're free. Ten thousand yen would be OK."

She took a business card from her purse. It had the name of a club and her picture on it, but the club's address and phone number had been crossed out with ball-point and only the cell phone number was left.

"I look much better with my make-up on. Ten thousand will do."

She grabbed the boy's arms, lifted him onto the carrier and rode away. He didn't look back.

6 When I heard the story from Ishikawa we were in an underground passage beneath a railway line. We'd taken several wallets, divided up the money in a booth in a bar and left, but he wouldn't let me go. He headed towards the indoor parking lot, then changed his mind and kept walking into the concrete pedestrian underpass beneath the railway line. Occasionally a bike would pass us, but at this hour of night the tunnel was quiet. Coffee cans and the wreckage of rotten lunch containers lay beneath the graffiti. Insects flitted in front of my face and I brushed them away with my hand as we walked deeper inside. The crunch of our footsteps echoed feebly under the low ceiling. Two small black plastic bags lay in the middle of the passage, their contents mysterious. When I touched one with my foot it sprang back with unpleasant elasticity, like dark meat.

"Not exactly the nicest place, I know," said Ishikawa, leaning against the wall. "That bar would probably have been fine, but maybe outside is better."

He'd drunk more than usual that day. He faced me and opened his mouth to speak, then looked at the ground. He lit a cigarette and took a couple of drags.

"I'm working for this company." He wouldn't look me in the eye. "No, maybe it's not a company. Anyway, whatever it is, I'm working for it. Maybe."

I squatted down and lit a cigarette of my own. The tails of my coat were almost touching the floor so I tucked them between my bent legs and rested my back against the wall.

"But it's risky, as things stand. It's not just that I might get caught. There's a possibility I might even get killed—or worse. So I've got to get out. While I still don't know much."

"What are you talking about?"

"Just listen."

A homeless man appeared at the entrance of the passage, saw us and shuffled away.

"If I quit now, while it's just like a part-time job, I can get out. I told someone I wanted to leave Tokyo. They know me, they know I'd never talk to the cops. But somehow he heard about it. I would just have been one insignificant person leaving, but he wouldn't let it go."

"Who?"

"The guy you met at the office. Calls himself Kizaki, but that's probably not his real name. He's the boss of the company, or whatever it is."

I felt a vague sense of foreboding.

"You can leave, he told me, but join us for this job first. That'll make us even for the passport and all the other stuff, he said. Because I'm in a good mood, he said. Even said he'd give me a cut. Wherever I end up, I should always be grateful to him, he said."

"What's the job?"

"Armed robbery."

I went a little weak at the knees.

"What?"

"Not like that. More precisely, they need a bunch of papers. The target's an old man, a speculator, and it sounds like they're going to fake a robbery and take the papers along with the money. They'll be pretty rough—when guys like these get impatient they generally are."

"What sort of papers?"

"I don't know."

I threw my cigarette butt into the gutter and stood up.

"It sounds suspicious. You better quit."

"Well, here's the real problem."

He paused. One of the lights in the passage, which had been flickering, gave up the ghost and went out.

"He told me to get you to come too. He knows about you."

"What?"

"You used to be in Tanabe's gang, didn't you?"

My heart started to beat faster.

"They would get their information sorted ahead of time and do the actual robberies. What type of keys the rich houses had, whether there was a safe. Real pros, completely different from those amateur outfits. The info came from somebody one of Kizaki's underlings knew. Of course the source's boss also took a cut. That's how Kizaki found out about you."

"This guy, what does he do?"

"I don't know. I thought he was a yakuza front man but somehow it doesn't look like it. How can I put it? He's weird, really weird. Talks a lot, laughs a lot, and there's a rumor that sometimes he kills people."

A young man in a suit entered the tunnel, muttering to himself. When he saw us he shut up, quickened his pace and disappeared out the other side. In his wake he left a strong smell of alcohol.

"Can't you do a runner?"

"Not easily. They say a couple of people have run away from him and ended up dead. He's relentless, I hear. He's like the yakuza in that way at least."

"You can't trust him."

A train passed over our heads, a freighter by the sound of it. I was nervous and I felt a throbbing warmth deep inside me. I knew that soon I would feel nothing but that heat. When the tower appeared in front of me, the dirty black plastic moved into clearer focus. I stared at the pathetic, flesh-like trash.

"But armed robbery means killing, doesn't it? I don't like—"

"No, it won't."

"Why not?"

"They want to avoid getting the cops involved. Even if he's robbed, the old man can't go to the police. The money comes from tax evasion and they'd be very interested in his papers as well. But if they kill him then it'll have to become a police matter."

"There's still something fishy about it," I said, but I decided to go along with it anyway.

I definitely had that pulsating heat in my gut. I was driven less by concern over what would happen to Ishikawa if I took off than by the presentiment that things were heading in a strange direction. In those days, whenever I was faced with a choice I favored action over inaction, the path which would lead me away from the world. As I walked behind Ishikawa, time hung densely around me. I felt as though I were being squeezed by something luke-warm and springy. Saeko's face drifted into my mind and when we emerged from the underpass I saw an iron tower

that I'd never noticed before. It stood there in the dark, its
tip exposed to the cold sky.

AT THE AGREED time Ishikawa brought Tachibana to
the station. I didn't know what their original relationship
was but sometimes he'd go pickpocketing with us and he
often watched us with a grin on his face. Without a word
we went into the office where Ishikawa always worked
on his own.

The desks and chairs were already gone and the room
was bare. We sat on the floor and immediately three men
entered. That made me even more nervous, because the
timing suggested that they'd been following us. Ishikawa
didn't seem to know them. They were carrying three large
cases, which they put carelessly in a corner as if they were
furniture movers.

"So you're the ones, are you?" said the tallest man in a
gruff voice as he sat down.

He appeared to be in his mid-forties, but his face was
covered in strange lines so it was hard to tell.

"Right, you guys look like you won't screw up. You all
look thoroughly dishonest."

He tossed us some bottles of water. I hesitated to open mine but Tachibana started to drink, watching their faces. The other two guys were in their thirties, of medium build. Like the tall man, their faces were marked with lines. One had a buzzcut, the other a flattop, and both were wearing dirty windbreakers.

"We're going to tell you the plan right now, and then we go through with it tonight. I know it's short notice, but we can't have anyone chickening out and mentioning it somewhere. Get yourselves ready. You get five million yen each. Any objections?"

The amount was inexplicably large. I glanced at Ishikawa but he showed no reaction, and neither did Tachibana. Looking at the man who was doing the talking, I decided to keep my mouth shut.

"Niimi's probably told you most of it, but the most important thing is that during the job no one says a word except for him."

While the tall guy was speaking the door opened and Kizaki himself came in. I was taken by surprise, but the other three men seemed to be shocked as well. He was wearing a black suit, a brand I didn't recognize,

sunglasses, and a watch on his left wrist. I couldn't iden-
tify the watch either. On his neck was a striking purple
scar. The tall man started to say something but he cut
him off.

"I've got nothing to do today," he said, face twisting in
what might have been a smile.

The men fell silent. In the hush that followed I could
hear the sound of my breathing. Their nervousness seemed
to be catching, and I stared at the man moving around in
the stillness. He appeared to stand out from his surround-
ings, to draw people's attention somehow. My skin tingled
where it was exposed to the air, as if he was emitting some-
thing. He watched us with amusement.

"So we meet at last," he said, curling his lip at Tachibana.

He seemed cheerful, a completely different person
from the one I'd met before in the same office. Tachibana
smiled back, trying to look cool, but he was sweating.

"All right, this is important." Kizaki turned to his sub-
ordinates. "It doesn't mean I don't trust you. So far you've
done everything I've asked of you perfectly. But I'm going
to talk to them now, because I'm at a loose end."

The three men nodded and he flopped himself down

in the space between us. My throat was dry and I sipped from my bottle. He was a little too close for comfort.

"The most important thing about carrying out a crime is planning. People who commit crimes without planning are idiots."

For some reason he looked at me when he said this.

"But because they're idiots in the first place they still commit the crime. They can't help it. On the other hand, really brilliant people don't care about the law either. In fact, without the law crime would be boring. Get it?"

He still didn't take his eyes off me. I didn't know what to say, so I said nothing.

"After that, it's all about courage. Do you know the book *Crime and Punishment*? Probably not. Raskolnikov, he had no courage."

Without turning around, he shifted position slightly and gave the flattop guy behind him a violent blow. I was shocked but tried not to show it. Flattop keeled over and as he lay on his side the man continued to beat him around the ear as though pounding his head into the floor. The harsh sound echoed. I kept my breathing shallow. My instincts told me not to move.

"That means that even if you see something unexpected like this you don't panic."

The guy who had been beaten picked himself up slowly and returned to a sitting position, his face swollen. When Kizaki turned back towards me his expression was unchanged but his breathing was somewhat ragged. I got the feeling this was caused less by physical exertion than by excitement. I looked away.

"OK, I'll put it simply. Maybe they told you already, but first of all, you two keep your mouths shut. We're going to the house of this old man, an investor. He's a perfect example of one of those pigs that the world spews out all the time."

I glanced at Flattop again. Our eyes almost met and I didn't know where to look.

In the aftermath of the violence Kizaki's low voice rang out clearly. He was wearing a business shirt of some kind under his jacket.

"You'll go by car, so you don't need to know the address, but you do need to memorize the layout of the house. It's really big."

The tall man brought out a plan. His hands were shaking slightly. None of the men seemed to have quite come to terms with the fact that Kizaki was there. Neither the guy who had been attacked nor Buzzcut moved a muscle, as though they had been turned to stone. They just stared at the man's back, sweating.

"There's the old man and a woman living in the house. She's his housekeeper and his mistress or something. His wife isn't there. That means there are only two people. There used to be two other women like that, but they both got pregnant and quit. There's a secretary as well, but she's on holiday overseas this week. Your job is to intimidate the woman and tie her up so that she doesn't get in the way. To assist, in other words. Only Niimi will threaten her, talking like he's Chinese. You've been told how to do that, right? Because you're used to armed robbery as well."

The man looked at Ishikawa and curled his lip. Ishikawa nodded briefly.

"Of course the mistress is a real looker, but don't get any ideas. I guess you're not starved for women. If you're horny, with five million yen you can screw as many women as you like. Yeah, we're paying you five million. Any objections?"

It was the second time I'd heard that, but I shook my head anyway.

"The gangsters around there are all morons. Can't use them. If they see a woman they can't control themselves. They'd leave semen and saliva, and if they just killed her she'd put up a fight and there'd be skin under her fingernails."

The three men laughed a little, as if in response.

"They'd get stupid ideas about the money as well. But I don't think I have to worry about you. You're not dumb, and I heard from Tanabe that Nishimura never gave them any trouble about the split."

I did my best to keep a poker face but couldn't prevent a flood of sweat. That was my real name. I'd never told it to Tanabe or Ishikawa or anyone. I tried to look at Ishikawa but couldn't catch his eye.

The man turned to Tachibana.

"You I don't know, but I guess you'll do. You're ambitious. I can see it in your face. An ambitious lad isn't going to risk his life for that sort of money. Anyway, here's the plan. The woman's bedroom is here. According to our listening devices, the old man calls the woman to his bed but never goes to hers. So as soon as you get inside the house you three go to this room and tie her up. If she's not there, go straight to the old man's room and do it there.

You don't have to deal with the old man. Just concentrate on taking care of the woman. Whatever happens, don't let her scream. Easy."

The man was sighing more frequently, as if he was getting sick of talking. The tall man tried to take over but he held up a hand to stop him. As he did so I could see the mark on his neck more clearly.

"In fact, this scheme is really interesting. I wish I could join you. In his safe the old man's got eighty million yen he's been avoiding taxes on. Apart from that, there are some papers in there that we need. The others will threaten them and make him open the safe. You don't have to do that, and if you can it's probably best not to look. But that might be impossible. Most guys can't help looking at money, just like they can't help looking at a beautiful woman. You'll use Japanese swords to scare him. Guns don't look realistic, and for scaring someone in a hurry cold steel is best. We'll give you the rope to tie her up afterwards. It's the same type as a gang of Chinese burglars used a month ago. You'll be wearing clothes and gloves and socks that are only sold in China. One of them was actually worn by a Chinaman in that gang. These guys will cunningly snag that piece of clothing on a door so they leave some fibers in the room. You'll have special full-face helmets so you don't drop any eyelashes. We've got two kinds of shoes—one set with the soles sanded off, and some with the same sole pattern as the ones the Chinese gang were wearing. That whole gang has already been taken out by some guys in Shinjuku. Even their bones are gone. If the old man self-destructs and decides to report the tax evasion and documents to the police, they'll still have to go to a lot of trouble just to get as far as that Chinese gang. And since they're already dead, the investigation will hit a dead-end. We're going to make them think that the crime was committed by people who no longer exist. That's one condition for a perfect crime.

"There won't be any killing, so you can relax. If you kill someone the cops take it really seriously. They put a lot more people on the case. There's no need for us to do anything dumb like that. It's better to leave the old man and the woman alive, use them to provide misleading information to the police. And most important of all, he doesn't know that what we're really after is that packet of documents."

He took a deep breath.

"There's not one thing that can give us away. The job's going to go off perfectly, so you could say that it's already been determined that in a few hours time he's going to lose his papers and his money. Even if you guys mess up and leave some evidence behind, there's nothing linking you to us. As of today this office will cease to exist and anything connecting it to us has already disappeared. If you're arrested and talk, all you can tell them is that you were working with a bunch of mysterious strangers. In fact, that's the truth. Still, if you do decide to help the cops with their inquiries, unfortunately for you armed robbery will only keep you in prison for so long. You can't be protected by walls forever. What's more, we've got friends on the inside as well. Even if you manage to defend yourselves against them and get out safely, you'll die as soon as you do. Not kidnapped and murdered by some shady characters. You won't die like that. Stabbed without warning by a woman in a crowd, shot from long range, knifed by someone who just happens to be riding the same elevator as you. That sort of death.

"In other words, what you guys have to do is not make

any mistakes. Don't get caught. Then accept the money with thanks and be quietly grateful to me. That's all."

His mouth relaxed and he lit a cigarette. A hush fell in the empty office; the clicking sound of the tall man unscrewing the top of his water bottle seemed very loud. Watching him smoking, I wondered why I'd never smoked in this room. Flattop's face looked puffier than it had before. Tachibana took a small breath, opened his mouth as if he was about to protest. Ishikawa remained silent.

"Um, I've got a few questions, just to make sure," Tachibana said. "First, whether the vehicle we'll use is safe. How we'll open the lock on such a big house. Then, when we'll get our cut."

The man cleared his throat and stubbed out his cigarette with a bored expression. He waved his hand and the tall man answered.

"The car is a van, stolen, and we got an expert to change the VIN. Even if we do get stopped at a checkpoint, my forged driver's license matches the car's registration papers. And if they write down the number on the plate, officially the car doesn't exist so there's nothing leading to me. More important, we know exactly where all the traffic checkpoints are today, and the location of the speed cameras. What else was there?"

"The lock. No, when's the split?"

"We'll give you your share in the car after it's all finished. That's safer for you than setting up a meeting later. We've already got a copy of the key. It's a really tricky door, and we can't afford to make a lot of noise opening it at night."

The man stood up and the other three got up to see him off. I wanted to ask why they couldn't do the job on their own, why they were bothering to use us, but I couldn't.

"Got it?" asked the man, but it was clear from his voice that he'd lost interest. "Remember, not all crimes are the same. A robbery with no plan is the height of stupidity. The profit is small, the risk is great. That's what these guys were like, but I taught them my system properly. If you understand the cops' methods and apply them in reverse, obviously you come up with an M.O. where you won't get caught. The important thing is the plan. Instead of sneaking around on worthless jobs, use your heads. Of course you'll go to the old man's house now, because those are my orders. Pay close attention to everything that happens during the robbery and enjoy it. You're going to get a taste of something that most people will never experience in their whole lives."

7 At one in the morning we climbed into a van and changed inside. As we put on the clothes, which somehow fitted us perfectly, the sharp smell of body odor filled the interior. The other guys lifted the mat from the floor and opened a black hatch.

"The swords are in this seat here," said the tall man as he stuffed our clothes into the hole. "We can put drugs in here, anything. We can even use it for people."

We waited for a while. Finally the door opened and a man I'd never seen before got into the driver's seat. He nodded briefly to the others and started the car. Threading our way through the narrow streets, stopping occasionally at traffic lights, we drove through the darkness of the city.

We smoked without speaking, staring blankly out the windows. My eyes idly followed a man on a bike. I noticed how well dressed a middle-aged couple in a car next to ours were. Christmas was approaching and the lighting displays on the houses were striking. Shiny Santa Clauses clambered up walls and every house glittered with rows of red and green and blue lights.

"He's just the driver," the tall man explained. "So when he's dropped us off he's going to hide the car somewhere for a while. We can't leave a suspicious vehicle parked in front of the house. If everything goes well, I'll call his cell and he'll bring it back. We'll get the money and when I give the signal you come back to the car first with these guys. I've got a few things to tidy up afterwards so they can't report us straight away, like tying them up and cutting the phone lines. Anyway, we have to be quick."

We went over a railway crossing and made our way quietly up a gentle slope. The surroundings gradually grew darker as we left the houses with their competing Christmas illuminations behind. When the tall man said, "There it is," I looked up and saw a large new two-storey building. Its design emphasized its overall squareness and made me think of a trendy office block. The garden wasn't all that big but the trees in the lawn were mismatched, as though they'd been picked up and planted willy-nilly. It was the old man's Tokyo house, the tall guy explained. The neighborhood was full of similar wealthy houses, and the paths and streetlamps were similarly well maintained.

We put our helmets on inside the van and were handed swords sheathed in identical scabbards. They weren't your typical Japanese swords, just crude oversized kitchen knives, with no dignity or elegance, solely designed to inspire fear. Kizaki's men checked the area as the car crept slowly forwards, then came silently to a halt.

"I'll go first and open the door," whispered the guy in the green windbreaker, who hadn't said a word the whole time. "Remember, Niimi is the only one who talks. You two keep your mouths shut."

He got out of the car, put the knife in his belt, carefully opened the gate and walked to the entrance. At that moment the porch light came on. I gasped, taken by surprise. He was trapped in full view in the middle of the garden. Tachibana started to say something but the tall guy held up his hand to stop him.

"It's just a light," he said. "It's only the light that comes on. We checked the house thoroughly. It's not connected to anything. There's no one around, so it doesn't matter. It's just a security gadget."

Buzzcut put the key in the lock, opened the door a fraction and waved. We all climbed out and walked in a black line through the brightly lit garden to the porch. I remembered the dry throat, the tension I felt long ago in my cat burglar days. The van started to move quietly away. The tall man made sure that we were all inside and then closed the door softly.

A black hallway stretched away from the entrance, cold and still. I recalled the thrilling sense of being out of place that comes with entering someone else's house without taking your shoes off. I followed Tachibana and Ishikawa down the corridor to the woman's room before the bathroom at the rear. The old man was probably in his own bedroom on the second floor. The others climbed the stairs slowly and vanished into the shadows. We were supposed to tie the woman up and take her up to the old man's room.

We stopped outside the wooden door and took a deep breath. Ishikawa eased it open and we went inside. The room was big and dark, but a shape was visible in the bed in the corner. Ishikawa moved closer, holding the duct tape, which he had already cut into lengths. If the woman fought back, he and Tachibana would restrain her while I threatened her with the sword. I gripped the scabbard, holding my breath. Ishikawa was used to walking without making a sound. Just as he was about to stick the tape over her sleeping mouth, Tachibana stepped on something. There was the harsh sound of cracking plastic, and I turned towards him. From the bed I heard her low, indistinct voice. Ishikawa put his hands on her head and over her mouth and whispered something in her ear. She nodded several times, but her body struggled instinctively, emitting harsh breaths and faint moans before finally growing quiet. Ishikawa switched on the bedside lamp and Tachibana drew his sword gently so she wouldn't panic. The woman looked at his long blade, at Ishikawa's arms, at me standing by the door. At Ishikawa's prompting she got out of bed, breathing violently through her nose. She was wearing nothing but a camisole, with no underwear. Ishikawa made her sit in the center of the room and tied her hands behind her with cord.

She was beautiful, tall and slender. With her arms bound, her breasts moved noticeably beneath her camisole. She was squirming with terror, long legs stretched defenselessly in front of her. Fearful for her life, she had forgotten her body entirely. All her curves were completely exposed, giving off a scent of perfume. In her fear and peril her body drew our attention like moths to a flame, without her even being aware of it. In front of the light Ishikawa checked that her hands were secure, whispered to her again and then cut another length of tape and placed it over her mouth. This terrified, beautiful woman seemed to stand out from her surroundings, blocking out everything else. Images of Saeko flashed before me. After a while I realized I was staring and looked away.

I could tell that both Tachibana and Ishikawa were touching her no more than was necessary. Ishikawa covered her with a thin cotton blanket from the bed, and then grasped her bound arms and raised her to her feet. With her wedged between them they climbed the stairs. The strong smell of her shampoo mingled with the body odor of the unknown man's windbreaker I was wearing.

Light seeped from the old man's bedroom on the second floor. I could hear faint voices, and when we opened the door the light was glaring. The three men stood in the large room with their swords drawn. A gray-haired man was slumped on the floor like an insect, his arms trussed tightly with rope.

Kizaki's men looked at us and the woman for a moment and then turned back to the old man, talking to each other in Chinese. The old man watched them wide-eyed. They gestured to us and we took out our swords as well. The old man didn't say a word, just stared at us, his eyes bulging unnaturally.

"We're not going to kill you, so open the safe."

I noticed that the tall man wasn't speaking broken Japanese, but rather feigning the slight accent of a foreigner who was quite fluent.

"Please. . . ."

The old man's voice was as hoarse as the cry of a wild bird.

"How many times do I have to tell you?"

"But if you kill me, you won't get the safe open."

He was making a feeble show of resistance, but his voice shook and he was drenched with sweat.

"My boss said he didn't care one way or the other. I can kill you or I can let you live. If I decide to kill you we'll take the safe with us, open it back at the shop. Makes no difference either way. Okay, I've had enough. Do it."

Flattop casually moved nearer, brandishing his sword.

"Don't get his blood on you. Cut his throat from behind."

"Okay."

The old man moaned.

"You really won't kill me?"

"That's up to you."

"Six five two two one star star zero five."

Buzzcut sat in front of the safe, which was built into a shelf in the corner of the room. He punched in the numbers and the door swung open. The tall man took out his cell phone, spoke briefly in Chinese and hung up again.

The safe contained far more money than the eighty million yen we'd been told. Tachibana made a noise like a cynical laugh in his throat. The tall man tossed a white bag to Buzzcut, who silently packed the money inside. When he picked up the bundles of paper and the envelopes, the old man whimpered.

"Wait! Just take the money."

The tall man said something to him in Chinese.

"Huh?"

"Yes, we're taking the stock certificates, title deeds and the other stuff too."

"No. Those aren't stock certificates. They've got nothing to do with you."

Buzzcut peered at the papers.

"*Wo kan bu dong*. I can't read this. I can't understand them."

"Honest!"

"Shut up."

The tall man gestured irritably to Flattop and the old man fell silent. The woman was still staring blankly into space. The old man struggled against his ropes, wriggling and swaying in confusion. When Buzzcut stood up with the bag he repeated over and over that they weren't certificates. The tall man pointed towards the door, so we left. As I walked out I saw that the woman was in a daze, no longer sitting primly but with her long legs sprawled out to one side. Her blanket had fallen off.

Flattop opened the front door and looked around. The rows of houses were still quiet. The van approached slowly and when he gave the signal we moved outside. In front of the gate the car door opened quietly. It had all been too easy.

"What about the other guy?" asked Tachibana, slightly hysterical.

I guessed he was talking about the tall man, who had stayed behind in the room.

"Wait for a bit. He told you, didn't he? He's tidying up a few loose ends. If they called the cops straight away we'd be in trouble."

As they were talking he came out of the house and climbed into the passenger seat. The van took off sedately, just as it had on the way here.

When I'd been in gangs before, after it was all over everyone would laugh from a sense of release. But these guys didn't say a word. Calmly they took off their windbreakers, put their helmets and the money bag in the space under the floor and stowed the six swords inside the seat, as if it was all in a day's work.

When they finished they sighed wearily. At that moment Ishikawa, who was sitting next to me, touched my fingers and slipped me a scrap of paper.

"Um," said Tachibana. "If it was that simple, couldn't you have done it on your own? I mean, why did you need us in the first place?"

I listened carefully for their reply, even though I was distracted by Ishikawa's note in my hand.

The tall guy lit a cigarette and spoke without turning round, as though he couldn't be bothered talking.

"We could have done it with three but it was better to have more, just to be sure. They'd feel outnumbered, and if the old man han't cooperated we would've needed several men to carry away the safe. What was the other thing you asked about?"

"Why us?"

"Actually we already had three other guys lined up. Friends of ours. But the boss changed his mind when he heard that Niimi was leaving town. To put it bluntly, you guys are kind of extras. He likes handing out money to punks like you."

I lowered my head, pretending to scratch my ankle, and

peeped at the slip of paper. It read, "Get out of Tokyo fast. Tomorrow 7 P.M., Shin-Yokohama Station, north exit."

"But still. . . ." Tachibana said.

"Persistent prick, aren't you? I don't know what he's thinking either. Anyway, you guys are lucky. Like he says, you should disappear and be grateful. There've been lots of things stranger than him hiring you for this. They were all his idea. One thing I know, though, when he tells us to use someone, they've never, ever screwed up. When I saw you I was sure you'd be okay. I guess he wanted to get Niimi to do one last job before he quit, give him a bit of money. Doing him a favor, you know? There've been guys like him before, but not that many. He likes young people. He's not going to do anything to you. It's not like he's going to be crapping himself over a few two-bit hoods like you running round. Even when he helped Niimi in Pakistan, from his point of view that was just a game. The plan for this job was perfect from the beginning. Tying up some woman and making sure you keep your mouths shut isn't exactly difficult. At any rate, you got lucky."

He stifled a yawn and put out his cigarette. Soon the van passed through a dark alleyway and emerged at an abandoned factory.

"This is far enough. Pull over."

They got out of the car and started changing their clothes. I saw ribbons of tire lying scattered like tender strips of meat, a rusting, tumble-down prefab, a white truck with broken windows. I moved slightly away from the men while I changed, but Ishikawa didn't take the hint. Without a word he removed his disguise and put on his own clothes.

"I'll pay you."

When he said this, Buzzcut opened the van door, climbed in and came out again, casually holding a bundle of money.

"Five million yen. No objections? It was easy, eh? I mean, this is frankly a waste."

He handed the money to each of us. The tall man yawned and the driver rubbed his eyes.

"We'll drop you off on the road somewhere so you can grab a taxi or whatever," the tall man said. "Niimi, would you mind taking over the driving for a while? He and I haven't had any sleep all night. We're likely to have an accident."

The car passed through narrow streets lined with houses and came out on a highway. The tall man and the driver were dozing off, so Buzzcut gave directions and told Niimi where to stop. I had no idea where we were. Apart from a convenience store way off in the distance there were no shops to speak of, and the gaps between the street lamps were wide and gloomy.

"Hurry up and get out. Hide the money in your clothes. You're pickpockets, so I guess you've got secret pockets and stuff. Anyway, I don't think you're stupid enough to be picked up by the cops."

Tachibana climbed out and I followed. Ishikawa started to get out too, but Buzzcut stopped him.

"Sorry, could you drive for a bit longer? These guys are out to it. We've got to go to Shinagawa to get rid of the car. Could you take us halfway?"

"No, I—" began Ishikawa, but Buzzcut laughed.

"You guys are so jumpy. OK, just as far as Kannana. I'll drive from there. Real pain in the butt, though."

I looked at Ishikawa. He nodded slightly, so without a word I watched the door close in front of me. The van moved off, gradually picking up speed, and before long it disappeared into the darkness. The area abruptly went quiet.

Tachibana and I stood for a while in silence. I stared

vacantly at the occasional passing car and smoked, thinking about Ishikawa. When I told Tachibana about the note that he'd passed me, he lit another cigarette.

"Get out of Tokyo, right?" He smiled faintly. "You know, he's too chicken. It was all cool, wasn't it? Anyway, I'm not hanging round here. I've got people to meet, women to fuck."

"I think I'm going to leave."

"Do what you like. But that was fantastic. It was easy and we won't get caught."

He stopped talking, seemed to be thinking about something.

"Who is that guy?"

"Who cares? Kizaki or whatever his name is? Anyway, it's best not to know. Just like he said. We should be quietly grateful."

We walked to the convenience store to call a cab. As two taxis pulled up in the parking lot, Tachibana threw away his cigarette butt in a ceremonial gesture.

"Well, I'm sure we'll meet up again," he said. "Guys like us are bound to meet again sometime."

• • •

I WENT STRAIGHT to Shin-Yokohama by cab. The city was blurry and the buildings and the people walking along the empty streets seemed to be floating in the blue dawn light. I got out of the car and went into a business hotel in front of the station. The woman at the desk went on and on about there only being a few hours left until checkout time. I told her I didn't mind paying for two nights, handed over the money and went up to my room.

When I lay on the bed I realized my body was still tense. I couldn't shake the feeling that I was still in the car, and at the same time that I was still in the old man's room. It didn't look like I'd be able to sleep so I thought about calling a hooker, but I didn't think I'd be able to find anyone to send me one at this hour. I lit a cigarette and wondered what would happen to me next. I couldn't stop thinking about what I was going to do and what I was going to live for. I saw images of the bound woman in the bedroom, and I thought of Saeko once more.

I HARDLY SLEPT all day. Seven o'clock, the time Ishikawa had given me, crept closer. Crowds of people were milling around the north entrance to the station. Looking at them, all with far more energy and vitality than my sleep-deprived self, gave me a mild headache.

Eight o'clock passed, then nine, but Ishikawa didn't show. I sat there, smoking nonstop. Under the neon lights the colors of the people's clothes hurt my eyes. I looked at a couple laughing boisterously, I looked at a businessman leaning against the wall, I looked at my watch, I looked at my shoes. I looked at a man walking towards me with his hand raised, and then realized that he was waving to someone else. Just then an elderly homeless man came up behind me.

"No matter what happens after this," he said, looking me in the eye.

My heart started to beat faster. All around me thousands of people were smiling at each other, their faces indistinct.

"Keep a low profile if you still value your life. You interest me. Let's meet again sometime."

I stared at him. My breathing grew rapid, and I consciously tried to slow it down.

"Who are you?"

"It's a message. I got it just now from a dude in a suit."

He took a bottle of whiskey from his pocket.

"Is there more?"

"Ah, what comes after that?" He coughed and screwed up his face. " 'I've decided to let you go for now. Be secretly grateful to me wherever you go.' I think that was it."

I went into the station, bought a ticket at random and waited for the bullet train. A news item about a war was blaring from the TV in the waiting room. The screen changed and I saw the headline: Mr. XX, House of Representatives Member, Murdered. Above it was a picture of the old man we'd robbed.

"According to an eye-witness who escaped unharmed, the assailants appeared to be foreigners. They forced Mr. XX to open the safe and then killed him with a sword-like weapon. The metropolitan police have opened an investigation and are treating it as another burglary by a Chinese crime syndicate, which have been increasing in recent years. And in the Diet. . . ."

I found out later that the following day the private secretary of another politician had committed suicide. The director of a public corporation fell onto a railway line and was hit by a train, and the president of an IT company disappeared and turned up dead. Share prices made an abrupt and unusual jump, then fell sharply. A Minister resigned, citing health reasons, and soon afterwards another politician belonging to the same faction also died.

I left Tokyo that night.

8 Leaning against a dingy office block, I lit a cigarette, shielding it with my coat against the wind. I put my hands in my pockets, felt the cold air chill my neck and shoulders. Two middle-aged women in uniform, so similar they could have been twins, came out of the building and gave me a suspicious look as they passed. My fingers just wouldn't warm up, so I went into a convenience store and bought a can of hot coffee. I wrapped my hands around it as I walked towards the concert hall.

In the smoking area I pretended to check my email and smoked another cigarette. I sensed the bustle of a crowd of people and looked towards the doors just as the concert-goers came pouring out. Since it was a classical program, most of the audience was elderly and rich. Berlioz's *Symphonie Fantastique*, Elgar's *Enigma Variations*, stuff I didn't know much about.

I joined the people making their way towards the taxi stand, picked out the most elegant retired couple in the crowd. Walking slowly, I moved closer, flexing my fingers in my pockets. They were looking at each other happily, praising the French conductor, talking about possibly going to hear him in France next time. The man wore a heavy brown Loro Piana jacket, and she was wearing a thick cream coat and a Gucci scarf. The man suggested they buy a present for their grandson and she smiled in agreement. In the afterglow of the concert their faces were filled with goodness, brimming with satisfaction at the beautiful music they had just heard. The soft lines on the old man's face showed that their lives had arrived at this point without a single wrong turn or false step.

His wallet was probably in the inside pocket of his coat, so I thought I'd have to take the orthodox approach, bump into him from head on. But then he said he was hot, slowed his pace and began undoing his buttons. I placed myself right behind him, using my own body to block the view of anyone following. I had to get it done before his wife started to help him. Just as he finished with the buttons and began to open his coat, I stretched out my hand at an angle, coming at him from his left. I slid my index and middle fingers into his pocket and grasped the wallet. At that moment it was as though my fingers could feel his genial expression and their easy lifestyle. I lifted the wallet and slipped it up my sleeve. As I passed him on the left he was struggling with his jacket. His wife said something to him and extended a slender arm to assist.

His wallet held 220,000 yen, several credit cards and some small photos taken with his grandson. The smiling boy standing between them and making a funny face looked really happy. I stuffed the wallet violently into a mailbox as though rejecting everything it stood for. A lightning rod glittered silver on top of the row of office blocks. It rose straight up, catching the rays of the sun. I looked away and plunged into the crowd once more.

• • •

I CAUGHT A cab and got out near my apartment. A small boy with long dyed brown hair came sprinting out of the shadows of the decaying apartments on the other side of the road, shouting. I passed rusted signboards, looked vacantly at shuttered-up shops next to concrete walls covered in graffiti. I thought about having a smoke but then changed my mind. I still wanted something in my mouth, though, and at that moment my fingers closed on a packet of chewing gum in my pocket. A car drove by right in front of me, accelerating as it went. I wasn't sure if it was gum I'd bought ages ago and forgotten about or if I'd lifted it when I got the coffee.

I lit a cigarette after all and wrapped my coat around me, trying to compose myself. When I came out onto the main street, among the sluggish passers-by I saw the kid who'd been shoplifting with his mother. He was alone, carrying the same paper bag and going into the same supermarket. I considered going home, but after hesitating for a few seconds I followed him in.

He was wearing blue shorts and a green windbreaker, but the fabric was shabby. After walking to the meat section, he paused briefly and then as quick as a flash seized some sliced meat and stuffed it in the bag. He chose the nearest packet and his movements were seamless. I felt as though the course of his life had been determined at birth, that he was constantly pushing against a powerful current.

Next he moved to the vegetables. Weaving his way through the cluster of housewives around the bargain bin, he used the blind spot they offered to pilfer some potatoes and onions. He was right-handed, and it only took him a split second to grab the goods and stash them in his bag. As I watched him I wondered which of us was more skillful at that age. But no matter how good he was, a child walking around a supermarket on his own stood out, and his choice of a paper bag was all wrong. A middle-aged woman pretending to be a customer was observing him, surely a detective hired by the store to catch shoplifters. It was a different woman this time, with long hair. She was tailing an old man who was acting suspiciously, but keeping her eye on the kid at the same time.

Unaware of her gaze, he stopped in front of the liquor shelves. He wavered, disconcerted, I was guessing, by the mismatch between what he was supposed to pinch and the size of his bag. The store detective's attention was locked on him. I had an image of hundreds of arms reaching out to seize him. I pictured him standing tiny and defenseless, bombarded by accusing glares and whispers of pity and shock, exposed to the world as "that kind of kid." I moved closer and stood beside him. Taken by surprise, he started to tremble slightly, keeping his face averted.

"You've been spotted," I said. "Dump the bag and get out."

He looked up at me helplessly.

"Same as before. You've been seen. Give it up."

I walked towards the woman who was watching. When she noticed me she looked away, bending down and pretending to be choosing some sweets. But the boy put three cans of beer into his bag, one after the other, and then trotted to the dairy products. There his head moved from side to side, searching for what he wanted to steal—or rather, what he'd been told to steal. I followed him. Checking that the woman wasn't looking, I quickly grabbed a basket and took his bag from him.

"That's enough," I said. "I'll buy it for you."

His first impulse was to fight back, but then he saw how much bigger I was and stopped. His face was dirty but his eyelashes were long, his eyes large and clear.

"What else do you need?"

He didn't answer. I saw a scrap of paper peeking from

his coat pocket, and I plucked it out and unfolded it. A shopping list, written in ballpoint. Untidy, slanting handwriting, probably his mother's.

I put the groceries in the basket and moved on. The boy came with me. The woman caught up with us and looked curiously at me, this adult who had suddenly appeared beside the child. Then she looked at the things in the basket and set off in pursuit of the suspicious old man, who had disappeared round a corner. The boy trailed after me passively, without even a show of resistance. Since I was dressed for work, my clothes were much flashier than his. Maybe he was ashamed that his pilfering had been spotted by someone like me. I turned to face him.

"You're good, but this is how you do it. Watch."

The only thing left on the list was yogurt. I stretched my hand towards the shelves where it was displayed, acting like I was trying to make up my mind. Glancing left and right, I caught the lid with my middle finger and tipped it into my sleeve. Sliding my hand to the left, I snagged three more containers. He watched my fingers earnestly and then turned and stared at my face as though he was seeing a miracle. He was clearly impressed that the yogurts didn't fall out when I lowered my arm.

"Now we buy the rest. Okay?"

Without waiting for an answer I went to the checkout and paid. We left the store and I transferred the purchases into his bag.

"You can't come back here. They've got a look-out and she knows your face."

The boy looked at me, one shoulder dragged down by the weight of the bag.

"Hiding things under the towel is a good idea, maybe. But you'd better stop. First, it doesn't look natural for a kid to be carrying a paper bag, so people notice. And it's small so you can't fit much stuff in it. Your moves—you go for the target too obviously. When you're shoplifting, you need to make some unnecessary movements as a diversion."

I saw that his face had turned serious and I looked away.

"Okay, take those and go home."

I walked away without looking back, chewing viciously on the gum I'd found in my pocket.

9 When I woke my neck and shoulders were drenched in sweat. I thought I'd been dreaming but I couldn't remember clearly. There'd been a tower in the fog, a long way off beyond the houses and the power poles. A stone tower that had probably been standing there for centuries, its surface carved in geometric patterns. It stretched straight up, dim and massive.

I smoked two cigarettes and thought of Ishikawa. When I ran into Tachibana I could have questioned him more closely, but I couldn't trust what he said. I didn't like the idea of being manipulated by his lies. The office where Ishikawa had worked had been turned into a beauty spa.

Suddenly I felt uneasy, like I had to get outside. I tried to decide where to go—the lounge of some high-class hotel, an exclusive brand-name shop, even Haneda Airport, where I'd thought about going before but changed my mind. I opened the door, planning to think about it as I walked. The boy was sitting in the cracked hallway. He seemed right at home in an old dump like this. He looked up at me blankly in the doorway, waiting passively.

"What are you doing here?" I asked.

He showed no reaction. I knew he'd been following me after we parted, but I never thought he'd come all this way. In his hand he held a brown paper bag, bigger than the one he'd had before. I think he knew that size wasn't the issue, though.

"What is it this time?"

He held out a piece of paper. It was a list in cramped, twisted writing on the back of a flier:

300g pork
ginger

lettuce

lotus root

carrot

3 x 500ml Super Dry

sliced squid

cup noodles (something you like)

Perhaps she was cooking for a male visitor.

"Impossible. These are no good for shoplifting. You should pick canned goods, processed veggies in packets, stuff like that."

He was wearing the same blue shorts and filthy green windbreaker, and he was rubbing at his leg with his right hand. I couldn't tell if he was doing it because of the cold or if it was unconscious, a deeply ingrained habit, but the movement of his arm was mesmerizing. When I went back inside for my bag he came in with me, still clutching his paper sack. Ishikawa would have laughed if he'd seen me now. I forced a brief smile. Then I hailed a cab, and as it pulled up the boy opened his mouth for the first time.

"Where to?"

His childish voice was high and pure, not yet worn down by his surroundings.

"You can't go back to that supermarket. They'll have their eye on you. We'll go further away."

I told the driver our destination and leaned back on the seat. For some reason the kid was staring avidly out the window at the passing scene as though he'd never seen anything like it before, his lips firmly shut.

WE ENTERED A giant supermarket in the basement of a department store and I got a basket. Then I picked up some sliced pork and slipped it in my bag, which was black with a slit hidden in the pattern so that I could put things inside without undoing the zip.

Once the boy saw my hand move he kept glancing at the bag.

"Grab the edge of my coat," I told him. "Pretend I'm your father and stay right beside me. Your body will help hide the bag."

I put a couple of packed lunches into the basket as camouflage while I filled the bag. This time the store detective was a woman in glasses, close to retirement age. The basket of her shopping cart was loaded with stuff so she'd look like a normal customer, but since she had to be on duty for a long time there were no perishables among them. She was keeping an eye on a woman in her forties with dyed brown hair who was walking along the aisle, her long white down jacket swinging from side to side.

"Stay there, but watch that woman."

Holding her basket in one hand, the woman in the white jacket quickly shoved a box of chocolates in her pocket. The security guard missed that one but kept following her as though she was sure the woman was up to something. They disappeared around the corner.

"Probably she's sick."

"Sick?"

"Stealing stuff without realizing it. There are people like that."

I was careful to keep my expression neutral.

"Maybe it's Pick's disease. That's also called early-onset *dementia*. But it's strange, a complete mystery. Why does the subconscious mind make people steal? Why does it have to be stealing? Don't you think it's something deep-rooted in our nature?"

The boy shook his head to show that he didn't know.

"But now's our chance. It's crowded and that store detective isn't here."

I put everything that was on the list into my bag, and beer, water and ham into the basket. Then we paid at the checkout and left.

WE WENT TO a park, and when I handed the boy one of the lunches he started eating without a word. I passed him a bottle of water but he barely touched it. Meat, omelet—he shoveled the food down so fast I thought he'd choke.

I opened a beer and chewed some ham. Dirty clouds were gradually closing in, blocking the light from the sun. In the distance a group of children clustered around a bench with Gameboys in their hands, all focused on the screens.

"As a kid, you have to choose what to take when you shoplift," I told him. "Otherwise it's too hard."

He looked at me between mouthfuls.

"Sweets, or at most soft drinks. It's pretty hard for you to take veggies from a supermarket."

I touched his windbreaker.

"What you could do, for example, is sew a pouch inside your jacket. Then you make a hole in your pocket so that it opens into the pouch. Or you can make a slit along the zip in the front so that it's hidden by the flap. You put every-thing in the pouch, and you stop before it gets too full."

Before I knew it he'd finished his lunch.

"Or a bag. A school bag is too conspicuous. A satchel like you would take to cram school is good. If you make a cut in a bag like the one I was using, you can put all sorts of stuff in. Then there's stealing. Wallets."

"I've done that."

He was watching the gang of kids on the other side of the park.

"On a crowded train with my mom."

"Really?"

"This wallet was sticking out of an old guy's pocket. I thought it looked like I could take that, I wondered if I could take it, and I took it. It had seven thousand yen in it. I've done it a few times since then. On trains by myself."

"Let's try it."

I put my own wallet in my back pocket and stood up. He bumped my left leg, as if by accident. Shifting his weight to his left, he took my wallet with his right hand.

"Not bad, but you should stop. I mean, it's still just for fun and you're not used to it. Anyway, you really do it like this, with two or three fingers. You don't use your thumbs like that. I guess you can't help it, though, since your fingers are short and you still don't have much strength."

I finished my beer.

"You could use a tool. It's got a tip like a fish-hook to snag the wallet."

"Have you got one?"

"I don't use tools. But there's a famous pickpocket who did."

"Who?" he asked, staring at me.

"A man called Barrington. An Irishman who lived in England a long time ago. He was in a theater company that was invited to noblemen's houses, and he picked those rich people's pockets like there was no tomorrow. He made the tools himself and was really good with them. He stole from ambassadors and Members of Parliament, even disguised himself as a priest. They call him the Prince of Pickpockets. He was brilliant, they say."

"Anyone else?"

"Well, you probably don't need to know about them."

"Huh?"

He looked at me in surprise. Then he seemed embarrassed, as if he'd chattered too much, even though I was the one who'd been doing all the talking. His skinny legs poked out from his shorts and his shoes were covered with dirt.

"There was also this eccentric who'd put a card with his own name on it in the wallet he'd lifted and then put it back. A famous American pickpocket called Dawson. And an amazing man, Angelillo, who's estimated to have stolen a hundred thousand wallets. A woman called Emilie was arrested for picking pockets and in the middle of her trial she pinched the judge's glasses case. Apparently the whole court burst out laughing."

The boy's mouth twitched slightly.

"What about in Japan?"

"There was a really good one called Koharu. In the old days coin purses were popular. They had a clasp that would snap shut like this. Some people wore them hanging on a cord around their neck. This woman Koharu could undo their coats and take the money from inside the purse. A technique called 'nakanuki.' What's more, the story goes that after she emptied the purse she'd close it again and button up their coat. Incredible skill."

"Really?"

"Surrounded by misery, those people laughed at the whole world."

Seeing the time on the big clock, the kids put away their games and left the park. A young couple went by, walking a dog. A little girl holding her mother's hand was looking at us and saying something.

"There's also someone who took ten million yen in one day."

"Ten million yen?"

"Yeah, a guy I know. He's dead, probably."

The boy looked up at me. I remembered my last glimpse of Ishikawa's face nodding at me, and the van's red tail lights disappearing down the street.

"People like that generally come to a bad end. So don't follow them. It's not worth it."

I showed him the 220,000 yen I'd taken from the old man with the grandson.

"I'm going to give you all of this. Next time you're told to go to the supermarket and steal, use this cash to buy the stuff. Don't come and see me again."

"Why not?"

"I'm busy."

I stood up from the bench. The boy walked in silence, moving closer to me and then moving away. When we parted he still didn't say a word. By the time I got home

I felt a chill. Even getting under the duvet didn't warm me up, and I figured I'd caught a cold. Going out to buy medicine froze me even more, but I took some drugs and tried to sleep.

I spent most of the next two days huddled under the covers. The ringing of the doorbell woke me from a dream of Saeko. I ignored it but it didn't stop. I couldn't tell if it was early evening or the middle of the night. I lit a cigarette, though I couldn't taste it. When I opened the door the boy's mother was standing there.

10

She was wearing a short skirt with black patterned stockings. She stared at me suspiciously and then peered into my room, her gaze moving back and forth in bewilderment, even though she had come here of her own accord. She fiddled with the button on her bag, her right eye twitching fiercely, and finally looked up at me searchingly. When she did that she looked just like her son.

"What do you want?" I said.

"Um."

Her eye closed tightly once more.

"You live in a place like this?"

"What?"

I realized it was raining outside and she was carrying an umbrella. In the drizzle a foreigner in work clothes was smoking a cigarette as he crossed the dimly-lit alleyway.

"I'm here because my boy said you gave money to him. A hundred thousand yen!"

Suddenly I'd had enough.

"You've come to give it back?"

"No way. I'm not giving it back. But why'd you do it?"

"No reason."

"It's kind of creepy, isn't it?"

No doubt it did seem creepy, but I couldn't believe that was her only reason for coming all this way.

"It's OK. Go home."

"Let me in. Or I'll scream."

She twisted her lips, trying to force a smile. I went back inside and she took off her boots, grumbling to herself. The way her right eye flickered, her nervous tension, reminded me of Saeko. When she removed her white half-length coat she was wearing a close-fitting white sweater that emphasized her breasts.

I swept aside a tangle of clothes with my foot, planning to sit down, but she planted herself in the space before me. Money was scattered on the ironing board in the corner, mixed with scraps of paper. I went and sat on the bed.

"What do you do for a living?" she asked, still inspecting my room.

"None of your business. Now what do you want?"

"Why did you give him that much? Was it for that?"

"What?"

"I mean, you must have done something to him. If I went to the cops you'd be in trouble."

She screwed up her face and glared at me as hard as she could. I grinned in amusement. She was too upset even to blackmail me properly.

"I'd never do anything like that."

"But there must be a reason. You can't fool me."

"It's because he looks like my dead son," I lied.

She looked away for a second, uncertain. I continued, saying the first thing that came into my head.

"He's the spitting image of my dead boy. I've got money,

but houses and stuff don't mean anything to me so I live here. I rent a bunch of places all over Japan. For me, a hundred thousand yen is nothing. I saw this poor kid shoplifting, so I gave him some money on an impulse. Like a donation. I was drunk. Anyway, you're the one who can't afford to go the cops."

"But. . . ."

She seemed to be thinking about something. She looked at the money tossed carelessly on the ironing board, then at the clothes in the closet.

"So you didn't. . . ."

"I didn't."

"But still. . . . Um, well, I wasn't absolutely sure that's what it was."

She looked down and then faced me again, as if she'd decided to take the plunge.

"In that case, be my client. Business has fallen off lately. My boyfriend spends money like water and I'm really in the shit. I need cash by tomorrow. I know I said before that ten thousand yen would do, but I need about fifty thousand straight away. He looks like your dead son, doesn't he?"

"I think I'll pass."

For some reason I sounded disgusted. She looked at

me blankly, her right eye firmly closed. She was breathing heavily through her mouth.

"Are you kidding?" she shouted suddenly. "Don't you fucking make fun of me!"

I was taken by surprise but tried not to show it. Unnatural wrinkles appeared on her face. She pounded the floor and made unintelligible gasping noises as if she couldn't control herself. Her emotions didn't seem to follow any predictable pattern. When I looked closely, I saw that her chin and shoulders were too thin for the rest of her body. Her neck and the backs of her hands were covered with red marks like she'd scratched herself.

"You were laughing at me. Like you can't have sex with a pro. It's not like I enjoy it. I haven't done anything wrong. You suck."

As I listened to her I felt something stirring inside me. My breathing quickened.

"No, I don't think like that. For one thing, I'm a pick-pocket. Can a pickpocket laugh at a hooker? Look, I—"

She was staring at me in amazement. I realized I was acting a bit strangely, so I lit a cigarette and tried to calm down.

"I really am a pickpocket, so I know what I'm talking

about. If the kid carries on shoplifting like that, he'll get arrested. If that happens the cops will be knocking at your door. Then you'll be in trouble too. So don't make him do it any more."

"But. . . ."

"If you need money, I'll give you what I've got here. About two hundred thousand yen. If I'm lucky, I can get that in one day. So don't make him."

"Really?"

Her tired eyes shone and she turned slowly to stare at the money as if I wasn't even there. At that moment she seemed to be lit by an overhead spotlight. Looking at her narrow shoulders, the curve of her body, the gentle gleam of her eyes, I felt a sense of panic.

"Take your clothes off. I've changed my mind. As payment."

She smiled faintly in satisfaction. Then she looked at my face.

"Okay, I won't make him steal anymore. And I'll make sure he eats properly."

Without hesitation she moved closer, taking off her sweater and undoing the hook of her skirt. Then she reached into her bag and took out some pills.

"These are great."

I held up my hand in refusal. She looked like she was about to say something so I lied again.

"Pickpockets can't do drugs."

AS I PUSHED her down on the bed I was thinking of Saeko. I'd spent a lot of time with her until four years ago. Even though she had a husband and a child, she frequently came to my place. She often told me she should never have gotten married. When we had sex Saeko used to cry.

Sobbing, panting, shaking, grabbing my hair, repeatedly sticking her tongue in my mouth. Thin but beautiful, her body would catch the light, seeming to pulsate all over. Her mouth opened in a swallowing motion as she cried, and then unexpectedly she would laugh fit to burst, as if she was expelling some unspecified emotion.

"Sometimes I want to destroy everything around me that has any value. I wonder why. I know it doesn't do me any good. Sometimes I don't understand what I'm trying to do. Is there anything you wish for?"

Saeko never looked at me when she spoke.

"You're a pickpocket, right? That's cool. But you don't do it for the money, do you?"

"Maybe the end," I said abruptly.

"The end?"

"What will happen to me in the end. What happens to people who live the way I do? That's what I'd like to know."

That time Saeko didn't laugh. For some reason she climbed on top of me without a word and starting making love to me again.

"I HAVE THIS dream. Even when I'm daydreaming, it's always the same."

Saeko told me this one month before she left me. We were lying on a bed under the red lamp of a hotel room, too lazy to get dressed, looking up at the walls and ceiling.

"It's somewhere way, way underground. I'm surrounded by old rotting walls and it's unbelievably damp. I'm falling, deeper and deeper, and at the very bottom there's a bed. A bed with no one in it. Since someone's put a bed there I know there's nothing beneath, that it really is the bottom. The bed has a hollow, and my body fits that hollow perfectly. As I lie there the hollow slowly starts to squeeze me, like you guys wrap me in your arms. As the hollow in the bed squeezes me, like it's comforting me, how can I put it, I get incredibly turned on. All sorts of conventional values are trampled and my body grows hot, like a flame, and I come again and again. I'm crying, laughing, smashing things, sticking out my tongue, and even though my body won't stop spasming it's like I'm still not forgiven. I pass out, then wake up again straight away. My outline becomes vague. I'm like gray smoke. But even in that state I'm still conscious. I can still feel every single one of those tiny gray particles and even beyond them so intensely that it hurts. And then I turn white with the heat. But at that moment this tall thing appears."

I looked her in the face.

"Long, glistening, towering. It's like I'm outside somewhere. Then as I'm looking at it I'm thinking, 'What is that?' It's pure, higher than the clouds, the top hidden from sight. And then I realize that I can't go there, that this hot smoky whiteness is my high point. But just because it's my peak, that doesn't necessarily mean that I'll reach it. What I mean is, it's my limit. It feels wonderful. I destroy all those values and I exist solely as sensation. I become unbearably hot and then vanish. That tall, shiny tower is a long way off, but I die happily under its ruins. Of course it's high and beautiful, and I can't help longing for it, but that's because it represents my greatest desire."

PERHAPS BECAUSE OF the pills, the woman cried out several times, digging her fingernails into my back, my shoulders, my stomach. After we finished she kept her tongue in my mouth for a while. I was still thinking about Saeko.

"Actual ruins, though," she had said to me once, "aren't abstract like that. Ruins are always boring. Solid, concrete and boring."

When the woman finally got off me, she lit one of my cigarettes and inhaled deeply. She moved close again and put her hand on my heart. The rain had stopped and everything was quiet. In the distance I could hear a shrill siren.

"Um, will you see me again?" she said, resting her nose on my shoulder. "It wouldn't have to cost this much, less would be fine."

"No."

"It was good, wasn't it?"

Her voice grew louder. For a second it seemed to blend

into Saeko's voice and I looked away.

"It was good, wasn't it? I bet it was. Absolutely."

"It's not that it wasn't good," I said. "You know they say that prostitution is the oldest profession?"

"The oldest? Hm. What's the second oldest?"

"Pickpocket. Stealing. That's the truth."

"Picking pockets is a profession?"

I grinned.

"I don't know, but if you're going to screw up your life, do it on your own. Don't get the boy involved."

The siren grew gradually louder and finally stopped somewhere nearby.

"Okay. I won't make him go shoplifting any more. I send him out when my boyfriend comes round. That's all right, isn't it? Sometimes he hits him, see."

"Hits him?"

"Not badly. Just a tap, when he's drunk."

"Anyway, shoplifting is out."

"Got it. But let's get together again, eh?"

She looked at her watch, put on her clothes and snatched up the money.

．　．　．

EVEN AFTER SHE left I kept thinking about Saeko. When she told me she couldn't see me any more, she was weeping.

"When I'm really fucked up—not that I'm not pretty fucked up now—but when I totally fall apart, then will you see me again?"

She certainly seemed to be serious. I didn't look away, wanting to hold onto her face for just a little bit longer.

"Next time we meet," I said, "I'll be more screwed up too. As bad as you."

Saeko smiled weakly.

"Yeah. I'd like that. Because you never look down on anyone."

But she died alone without getting in touch with me. She disappeared and when her husband found her she'd overdosed. She didn't leave a note.

The night I heard about it I went out in the street and stole indiscriminately from rich and poor alike. Burying myself in the crowd, I took wallets and cell phones, even gum and receipts and handkerchiefs. Breathing raggedly, with tension and pleasure running through me, I took them all. High overhead shone a white moon.

11

I ventured outside for the first time in ages. The wind was blowing a fine rain and everything looked blurry, like in a fog. I passed a group of foreigners in laborers' clothes, then a woman in an extremely short skirt talking loudly on her phone. I realized that the kid was following me but kept on walking, figuring that if I ignored him he'd give up. For no particular reason I was clutching my cell phone. I bought a can of coffee from a vending machine and warmed my hands on

it. My temperature had gone down but I still had a head-
ache. I drank the coffee and tried to decide where to go.

I thought checking out a nearby hotel or sneaking into a
function somewhere would be better than going to Haneda
Airport. In a convenience store I bought a magazine to
check out what was on. When I came out with my bag the
boy was standing in the parking lot behind a small truck
with muddy tires. I went into a run-down coffee shop to
read my magazine and to make him give up. The interior
was dark and damp with a low ceiling. I ordered a coffee,
even though I'd just finished one.

The waitress was wearing a short skirt and black stock-
ings. She reminded me of the boy's mother. Just then
he came into the shop. The glass door was wet from the
drizzle. Like me, he had no umbrella.

He sat down at my table. When the woman in the mini-
skirt came over with a smile, he asked for an orange juice.
I lit a cigarette and looked at his dirty clothes.

"Go home."

He ignored me. Then he spoke in a small voice as if he
was opening the conversation.

"She took my money."

"Yeah?"

"But only a hundred thousand yen. That's all she found. I've still got a hundred and twenty thousand left."

"Ah."

When his drink arrived he stared at it seriously, like it was precious to him, and stuck the straw in his mouth.

"I don't care," I said. "Go home. I've got things to do."

He went on drinking as though the orange juice was the only thing in his world.

"Show me how you do it."

"No. I told you. You'd get in the way."

He finished his drink and looked at my coffee, fiddling with the paper wrapper the straw had come in.

"I'll just watch from a distance. It can't hurt if I just watch, can it?"

"Nothing doing."

"Why not? If I'm a long way off, I won't be in the way."

He was a lot more talkative than before.

"If you don't like being at home, go to the library and read a book or something."

"Did you do it with my mom?"

The dim lights of the shop reflected off the surface of the water in my glass. I was a bit taken aback, but I kept my expression neutral. I breathed in slowly.

"Look, you know how it is. I'm not your guardian angel. I'm just like all those other guys."

"It's okay, I don't care."

He looked down, went on playing with the paper.

"I'm used to it. I've even seen them at it."

"But I bet you don't like it."

"It's gross. But. . . ."

He rubbed his thighs, started to say something else and then changed his mind. The ice in his glass had melted into the little bit of orange juice that remained, and he sucked it up noisily with his straw. A Christmas song was flowing out of the speakers.

"Better you than him."

"That's not going to happen."

"Don't you like her?"

"What about your dad?"

"I don't know him."

I wondered why I was bothering to ask him questions. I picked up the tab and left. The kid came with me.

WE CAME OUT the east exit of Shinjuku Station and walked under the neon signs, avoiding the main crush of the crowd. When I leaned against the wall of an office building and lit a cigarette, my eyes met those of a homeless man walking toward me. The boy looked scared and mover closer. He started to clutch at my sleeve but then thought better of it. I gazed at the herd of people streaming by while I smoked.

"People don't concentrate all the time. Every day they get distracted dozens of times."

"Yeah."

For some reason the kid had brought along the colored cardboard coaster from the coffee shop.

"If someone calls their name, for example, or there's a loud noise, most of their attention is drawn to that. Just like you were looking at that bum a second ago. There are limits to people's awareness. More exactly, they're sensitive when they're breathing in and when they're holding their breath, but when they breathe out they relax."

The boy glanced at my sleeve.

"Pickpockets know this and we take advantage of it. The classic technique is to take the wallet at the moment you bump into them. But actually picking pockets isn't a one-man job. You need partners. Three people is standard. One person to jostle the mark, one person to block other people's view, one person to lift. And jostling doesn't mean hitting them as hard as you can. Just brushing them with your shoulder is enough. In a crowd like this, if the person walking in front stops suddenly, the person behind will lose their balance, right? That's all you need. The person who does the actual lift stops anyone seeing him from the left, and the blocker shields the right and from behind. The one who takes the wallet immediately passes it to his partner, who hides it. If you do it like that you'll never get caught."

A host, a sleazy guy standing outside a ladies' bar trying to entice customers, was pestering a woman chatting on her cell phone as she walked. His ugly face was impossibly tanned, horrible enough to take your breath away.

"If you've got five people, two of them start arguing, and while everyone's focused on that the other three can steal the spectators' wallets. I've also heard of a street performer and a pickpocket who worked as a team. A long time ago, when I was teamed up with that guy I told you about, the one who took ten million yen, we used a whole range of tricks. He'd pretend to be drunk and put his arm round the mark. Then I'd step in to stop him and take their wallet. Or I'd trip someone up and run away. He'd steal their wallet while he was helping them up. Sometimes we paid some bum to shout that there was a pickpocket in the crowd. Every single person would instinctively put their hand on their wallet. We'd know exactly where each one was, so they were easy to steal. A kid like you couldn't get a wallet from inside someone's coat. You'd have to stick to the back pocket of their trousers. I don't like tools, but you could use a small blade. If you cut along the stitching of the pocket, the wallet would just fall out under its own weight. But anyway, the basic thing is how you're going to distract the target."

I started walking and the boy did too.

"Stay there. Just this once."

I followed the ugly host with my eyes.

"That guy's wallet is in his right back pocket. I'm going to walk up behind him and tread on the heel of his shoe. While he's off balance I'll take his wallet, moving in time with him. Of course there's a knack to treading on some-one's heel. You aim to hit them just as they're about to take the next step. That way, nine times out of ten they'll fall forward. Your own coat hides what you're doing from people around you."

I unbuttoned my jacket and approached the host. He

looked around, spotted a flamboyantly dressed woman and changed direction. I followed him, opening my coat slightly to block the view from the left and checking that there was no one on my right. Then at the same instant I stepped on his right heel and pinched his wallet between my fingers. As he toppled over I pulled it, my body moving in unison with his. Slipping it into my right sleeve, I muttered an apology and moved off as he turned around, pretending I was in a hurry. He started to say something, but then looked away and scampered after the woman. I walked round a corner, the wallet still in my sleeve, and the boy joined me.

"Did you get it?"

It was an entirely ordinary brown Louis Vuitton wallet.

"Eight thousand yen. That's pathetic. We'll throw the wallet in the gutter somewhere."

"I couldn't see it. But I kind of got what you meant about matching his movements."

"Really?"

He nodded emphatically.

"You're small, so maybe you'd be best to crash into him at full speed, like a kid would do. As soon as you hit him, take his wallet. Then you say sorry and run off again, same as when you ran into him. If you're on a train there's no way out if you're seen."

"I want to try."

"No way. Well, okay, try it on me."

We went into a nearby Marui department store and stood in front of the mirror in the toilets. I took off my coat and put my wallet in my back pocket. He bumped into me and lifted it between his index and middle fingers and his ring finger.

"Try again."

He repeated the same actions, took the wallet in exactly the same way. His timing was almost perfect, taking it at the exact moment I lost my balance. I figured he was about as quick as I had been when I was his age, and unless he made a mistake he wouldn't get caught.

"That's hopeless," I said.

THE STREETS WERE busier than before. Just as I was thinking about buying the kid some clothes, he mumbled that he was going home. I thought he was sulking, but he said quietly that if he was late he'd get hit.

"By your mom?"

"By that guy who's always coming round."

He was looking at me impassively.

"Sometimes, when he's drunk or whatever. It's like he's looking for an excuse to get angry, so I'll get in trouble."

I stopped a cab and handed him the 8,000 yen I took from the host. Before the door shut he asked in a small voice if he could come and see me again. When I replied that I figured he would even if I told him not to, he nodded. He even seemed to smile a little.

Watching the taxi drive away, I thought the man living with his mother must know about her job. Maybe he was the one who put her up to it. In the show window of a department store was a child-sized mannequin, all dressed up. Just as I was idly contemplating buying the outfit, I spotted a rich man on the other side of the street. I didn't have any cash on me, so I figured it was karma.

An image of Saeko's face flashed into my mind and I wondered what her child would be up to now. Her kid was probably about the same age as the boy.

I moved around so that I was facing the rich man I'd just seen, brushed against him gently and grasped his wallet with my fingers. Maybe I'd better buy lots of clothes rather than one good set, so that the boy could have changes. My heart skipped a beat as my wrist was seized. For a second I couldn't work out what had happened. I tried to break free but the fingers holding me were incredibly strong. My hand was locked completely rigid and I couldn't move a muscle, as though I was paralyzed. The people around us passed by without a glance. I was aware of the neon lights, the rows of cars, the huge buildings towering overhead. And right in front of me, squeezing my wrist, was Kizaki. He was wearing sunglasses, expressionless, his hair extremely short. Strangely, the scar on his neck was gone. All the other pedestrians just veered around us. I stared at him, unable to look away.

"Long time no see. I've been watching you."

I couldn't get my breathing under control. I had no idea what he was doing there.

"Niimi told me you guys only target rich people. I saw you from miles away, came closer and walked in front of you on purpose. It was brilliant. There's no doubt about it, I'm the richest person here."

12

With the man still gripping my arm tightly we passed through Kabukicho and entered a building standing in the shadows. He was so strong that I knew it was pointless to fight back or struggle. In fact, as we climbed the stairs in the darkness, I felt as though trying to escape would put me in even greater danger. The landings were filthy with dirt and grit and the grey walls were badly discolored, almost black in places. The exit was already far below us. Behind a door with no sign or nameplate we came to another door, a single sheet of black steel.

When he opened it we were met by a wave of noise and red light. Under the powerful glare was a writhing mass of men and women, their naked bodies squirming on tables and couches. An old man had his face buried between the legs of a woman sitting on a table, and I could hear another woman's cries of delight in response to a young man's thrusts. Several couples were humping on the sofas, their tongues in each other's mouths. Still holding my arm, the man made his way through them. My eyes met those of a woman with a guy's penis in her mouth. Behind her was another woman, mouth open, been fondled urgently by two handsome young men. A man dressed as a waiter stepped silently from behind the counter to lead us, paying no attention to the people around him. A woman groveling like a dog on the floor grabbed my leg, shouting something unintelligible. I brushed her arm away but she seemed unaware that she'd grabbed me in the first place, never mind that she'd been shaken off. I saw the sprawled body of a woman staring into space and a well-built man collapsed on the floor. We passed a woman being strangled, her head pulled back towards the ceiling, and a man being licked all over by a woman. One lone woman was having convulsions on the floor. Beyond her was another door. For some reason I was struck by the thought that Ishikawa might be here.

The waiter opened the door, crossed a narrow corridor and ushered us into a small room. Two couches faced each other with a low silver table between them. Apart from an Impressionist style painting of some fuzzy plants, the walls were bare.

"Something to drink?" the man asked, apparently indifferent to the scene we had just witnessed.

"No, thanks."

"Well, water then. And the usual."

The waiter bowed deeply and left, closing the door behind him. The noise was immediately muted and in the quiet room I heard a high ringing in my ears, as though someone was calling me from far away.

"This place is hell. Fascinating, isn't it?"

He took a cigarette from a case and put it between his lips.

"But it's a safe hell, because only people who've passed an STD check can join. Once you become a member, though, there's no getting out. Because it's hell. There's not one person who doesn't come back."

There was a knock at the door and the waiter entered. On the table he placed a tall glass etched with spirals, a bottle filled with what looked like whiskey, a clear glass and a bottle of water. Then he left and the room was silent again. The man sipped his whiskey, smiling, without saying a word. I poured water little by little down my sore, parched throat. He watched me, drumming his fingers on the table.

"This wasn't by chance, was it?" I asked, my voice still hoarse despite the drink.

The muscles at the back of my arms went slightly numb.

"Of course it wasn't by chance. I've known for a long time you were back in Tokyo."

"How?"

"I heard it from Tachibana. But even if I hadn't, I'd have found out anyway. Because it just so happened that I wanted to see you. I heard from a subordinate that you were in Shinjuku, and then I looked out the window and there you were. And when I went closer, voila! You came to me! Just like a true pickpocket."

"And Ishikawa?"

"He's gone. Without a trace."

I felt a dull ache in my heart.

"To be completely accurate, only his teeth are left. We burned his corpse and ground his bones into white powder. His teeth are probably scattered somewhere in Tokyo Bay. Too much trouble to crush them. It's not like there's a body buried some place. He has literally disappeared."

"So am I going to disappear too?"

"Didn't you get my message? That I was going to let you live? You could be useful and it might be entertaining. Him, he knew too much. Probably he didn't tell you anything, but he knew too much so he said he wanted out. I just got him to help with that robbery before I killed him."

My body went weak and for a second my eyes lost their focus. From behind his sunglasses the man seemed to be looking directly at me, unblinking.

"Why?"

"What?"

"Why didn't you do that robbery by yourselves? Why hire us?"

The man wiped his lips. Absurdly, it occurred to me that even guys like this wipe their lips.

"If by some chance in a million something went wrong with our plan and the cops didn't believe a Chinese gang was behind it, then we needed some dead bodies. Burglars' bodies. We planned to make you three into another team of imaginary robbers, separate from us, to make it look like you were working for a different outfit. If we killed people we've worked with before it would definitely lead back to me. Maybe not all the way to me, but close enough. If you were dead, though, all the cops could do was head in the direction we pointed them. You know why?"

I said nothing.

"Because you guys have no family. Because you're all alone in the world and even if you'd died there wouldn't have been a single person who cared. It would have taken them ages just to ID you. Faced with a bunch of corpses and no clues, the police would have swallowed the fake evidence we planted hook, line and sinker. So at the time I needed some loners, people with no attachments. Of course, since they had no attachments they could have run away from me. They had that freedom."

"That job." My voice shook slightly. "It wasn't really a robbery, was it? Maybe you needed the money and papers too, but it was really about murder."

"Yes. But that's not the whole story."

The man continued to smile, sipping his drink.

"I needed a death which the public and the media would think was just bad luck, a killing during a robbery. But a tiny group of people would recognize that politician's death as my handiwork. That was the point. The message wasn't just, 'If I cross him I'll be killed.' It wouldn't be a violent death that raised doubts, like being pushed in front of a train or shot dead. It would be assassination disguised as a run-of-the-mill crime. Everyone would take it for granted that they'd died during the course of an actual crime, as though they'd walked in on the robbers, with not a shred of doubt. That's got to be scary. Some people would think I'm powerful enough to get the Chinese mafia to work for me, others would think that I've got the criminal knowledge and systems to make it look like the Chinese mafia. Either way, it makes them afraid of me."

He moistened his lips with whiskey and moved his tongue inside his mouth as though softly stroking the inside of his cheeks.

"That politician, he was an errand boy for some powerful people, some major players in the underworld. He was in the way. And his death frightened the people who were reluctant to deal with us. Now they've agreed to do business. Of course they didn't tell us why they'd come round. They made up plausible excuses, like their boss finally gave them permission, or what the hell, profit comes first. But there were obstacles getting in the way of many of those dealings, and with the documents we got our hands on I could eliminate some of them. I knew that meant that several people would die, and I also knew that their deaths would make it even easier for us to operate. If this happens, then that happens, and so on. It's all a jigsaw puzzle. With the profit we made, the money we gave you was just small change. It's not just about profit. It's about power too. And this is just a sideline. It isn't even that important to me."

"Why did you let me live?"

"There was no reason to kill you. I told you, you might be useful. I don't need two pickpockets. Maybe if you hadn't turned up Niimi wouldn't have died. It all depends on my mood. And now, I want you to do something for me."

He looked at my face. I braced my legs, ready to stand up quickly.

"I won't do it."

My throat was tight and it was hard to breathe. Seeing he was about to speak, I started to rise.

"There's a kid you've made friends with recently, isn't there? Have you already done it with the mother?"

I could dimly make out the shape of his eyes behind his sunglasses.

"As a threat, that's kind of old-fashioned, isn't it?"

"Old-fashioned threats are the most effective," he said with a laugh. "You and Niimi are both pretty dumb. Even though you've chosen this lifestyle, you still seek attachments. That's the height of stupidity. You'd be much better off if you were truly free. The only reason Niimi didn't run away before the robbery was you."

"Niimi said that?"

"I gave him a choice—either you both took part in the job and I let you live, or if either of you tried to get away I would kill you both. If he was just out for himself he'd have thought about running even if it meant risking your life."

I went to light a cigarette, and then saw there was still one burning in the ashtray. The man was staring at the smoke rising from it.

"To put it plainly, you work for me now. You can't refuse, because if you do, the woman and kid will die a horrible death. It's your fate. Fate is like the relationship between the strong and the weak, don't you think? Look at religion, for example. The Israelites, who worshipped Jehovah—why were they afraid of him? Because their god was powerful, that's why. Everyone who believes in gods fears them to some extent. That's because gods have power."

He took another drink.

"Imagine that God wasn't the creator of the world but just a superhuman with superpowers. It would still be the same, wouldn't it? They'd obey him, worship him, pray to him for their own prosperity. I'm going to tell you a story. I'm in a good mood today."

He made a call on his cell phone and the waiter brought more whiskey and water. Without my noticing, I had finished my drink and my glass was completely dry. Still expressionless, the waiter bowed as low as before and left. People were still cavorting in the other room.

"A long time ago, in France when they still had slavery, there was an aristocrat."

He seemed to be getting drunk, but his swarthy complexion was unchanged. He looked at me with amusement, leaning back on the dimly-lit sofa and gesturing with his hands as he spoke.

"A thirteen-year-old boy was bought as a servant for the nobleman's castle. A beautiful boy. The nobleman was bored with life and looking for excitement. He spent his fortune freely and acquired whatever money could buy. He slept with different women almost every day. He lived like a king with power, fame, everything he could possibly desire."

He paused for breath.

"The nobleman looked at the youth and thought that he would try to prescribe his entire future. The story of his life, his joys, his sorrows, even his death, he would decide it all. Like Abraham and Moses, who were always under God's control. For one year he observed the boy's personality and abilities, forming a general impression of how he would react if the nobleman did this or that. He took some paper and started to write down the young man's life from that point on. It took him several days to write. The book outlined the young man's fate. What was in that book could not be changed. The boy would have to live his life exactly as it was written there."

Circles of orange light reflected off the man's shades.

"When the boy was fifteen he met a girl he liked, but before they could get together she was moved to a far-away place. They parted with floods of tears, like in a B-grade movie. It was the nobleman who'd brought the girl close to the boy, and of course it was he who separated them.

"At eighteen the boy was given permission to visit his parents, who were serfs, for one day only, but on that day the family was attacked by outlaws. Naturally that was all according to the nobleman's instructions, and had been written in his book beforehand. The boy's parents were slaughtered before his eyes. Apparently the noble spent the whole day sitting in his chair, heart pounding—not out of horror at what he was doing, but because he was worried that the brigands he'd hired might kill the boy by mistake. In his fury and heartbreak the young man's face lost its innocence.

"Then he was invited to learn swordsmanship with the noble's private army. It was impossible for a slave to become a knight, but he could go into battle. He could also join the pursuit of bandits. The youth became skillful with a sword. Of course the commander was also following the nobleman's orders. During the day the boy worked as a servant in the castle and at night he practiced the art of the sword, because in that wound that would never heal he had found his reason for living. Like Job when he was being tested by the Lord, he never cried out, why is this happening to me? He didn't realize that he was being manipulated by the nobleman.

"His master had also written many of the minor events in his life in advance. For example, he was seduced by a female servant and slept with her. The steward was going to punish him, but he was saved by a pardon from the nobleman. At that, the young man swore even greater loyalty. Even the trivial details of his day-to-day life occurred exactly as was in the notebook—the mistakes he made in his duties as a servant, the small rewards he received.

"At twenty-three he reached the high point of his life. In other words, the climax of the book. He took part in an outlaw hunt and found himself face to face with the men who murdered his parents. The captain ordered him to finish them off. Amusing, isn't it? With tears in his eyes, the young man killed the bandits. At twenty-six he married a woman slave on the nobleman's command, but she had such a troubled personality that he soon tired of her. Once again he was seduced, starting an affair with the nobleman's mistress, often meeting in secret. Of course that too had all been dictated by the nobleman, just as it was written in his book. Before long the nobleman's mistress became pregnant and the noble, who knew the whole story, casually told the young man that out of all of his children he wanted to make this one his heir. The youth was troubled and afraid.

"The noble even wrote a banquet scene in which the young man was waiting at table on a crowd of aristocrats. The mistress seemed to be on the verge of making a full confession but then changed her mind at the last minute. The nobleman was vastly entertained. And then, when the young man turned thirty, the nobleman summoned him to his chamber."

He stopped. I had a slight ringing in my ears and the revolving shadow of the ceiling fan was bothering me. He spoke briefly into his cell phone. I continued to smoke, and the man drank his whiskey.

"The nobleman handed the youth a bundle of papers bound with string. When he opened the pages, he saw his whole life until that point recorded there. It was what the nobleman had written some fifteen years before. It must have been a terrible shock when he saw it. At the end of the story, he was to be put to death in front of the nobleman for the crime of laying his hands on the mistress, even though that crime had of course been staged by the nobleman himself.

"The young man collapsed on the floor. It took him a long time to fit all the pieces together. At the instant he understood everything and looked up at the nobleman, trembling with emotion, the soldier standing behind him stabbed him in the back. I have no idea what thoughts were going through the young man's head before he died, but the nobleman was quivering with delight. He was enjoying an overwhelming pleasure, quite unlike fortune, fame, the joy of being with a woman. The nobleman savored that pleasure with a serious expression, as if transfixed, forgetting even to laugh."

I opened my mouth for the first time. "That's crazy," I muttered.

His smile didn't waver.

"It's not crazy. That nobleman was simply appreciating everything life has to offer."

"You made that up, didn't you?"

He laughed.

"No. To tell the truth, my lieutenant who planned the robbery made it up on the spur of the moment when he was drunk."

"With you as the model?"

"That's right. You catch on fast. In other words, from now on your life depends on me."

He drained his glass.

"I've got the notes to your future inside my head. It's extremely interesting, manipulating another person's life. Now I've got a question for you. Do you believe in fate?"

"I don't know."

"That's the most boring answer. Was the young man's fate really controlled entirely by the nobleman? Or was being controlled by the nobleman the young man's fate?"

There was a knock at the door. When Kizaki answered a thin man in a suit came in. He put an attaché case on the table, bowed and left. Kizaki opened the case and took out several photos and papers.

"You're going to do three small jobs for me. They really are trivial tasks. But if we use you, certain things we want to do will become much easier. First, steal this man's cell phone in the next six days. Put it in the mailbox of an apartment we'll tell you about. The guy's home security system is state-of-the-art, so it would be hard to break into, and for various reasons we can't kill him yet. As for why we want his phone, we need to find out who he's talking to, quickly and smoothly. We could attack him on the street and grab it, but in this case it's preferable that he doesn't realize it's been stolen, that he thinks he just dropped it.

"The second job is to take some small item, any item, from this man within seven days. A lighter would do. Some everyday object that will have his fingerprints on it. The point is that he mustn't know it's been stolen, just like the first man. The object will end up next to a dead body. Of course we're not trying to get him convicted, but by making the police suspect him, pick him up for questioning, various other things will be revealed. His room is hard to break into, too. And get some of his hair, as well as the lighter or whatever. It won't be easy, but do it anyway. I want two or three strands. Obviously they won't look natural if they're cut, so pull them out by the root, of course without him noticing. Put those in the mailbox, too."

Keeping my face blank, I gazed at the photos. The man was pointing at them gleefully, as if this were a game.

"Finally, I want you to steal some documents from yet another man. You've got ten days. We don't have a photo yet, but we'll get one. One of my men made it into his apartment but couldn't find the papers. It looks like he must carry them on him. He's a coward, extremely nervous. He also carries a gun. You have to steal the papers in such a way that he doesn't realize they're gone for at least two days."

"That's impossible."

"Impossible or not, you'll do it. The documents are in a sealed envelope, so maybe he doesn't know what's in it. Once the envelope is opened it will probably lose half its value. Replace it with this dummy, which we had made by someone on the inside. They real papers should be in an envelope from this company, and the confidential documents should be stamped like this. But we're not certain about that, so check before you make the switch. This can't go in the mailbox. Give it to me directly."

"And if I fail?"

"You die. Perhaps you think that's unfair, but once I've got someone in my sights, that's how it is. Don't worry, I won't kill the woman and her brat. Tension and a heightened sense of responsibility can stretch a person's abilities to the max, but if you apply too much pressure it can have the opposite effect and lead to mistakes. And where possible it's best not to create unnecessary corpses. The more dead bodies you leave lying around, even if it's only one or two, the greater the chance is that things come to light. I only killed Niimi because he knew too much about my core business. I don't murder people for no reason. I'm not just talking about you—that's why I didn't kill Tachibana either, even though he's not much use to me. But if you refuse, then I'll have no choice. I will kill the boy and his mother. It'll mean more work for me, but that's how I operate."

He put the papers and photos back in the attaché case and pushed it across the table. I had to take it.

"I direct other people's lives from behind a desk. Reigning over people like that—that's like being a god, don't you think? If there is a god, he appreciates this world more than anyone. When I'm controlling people I sometimes feel like I've absorbed them. Their thoughts and everything they've ever felt are inside me, like I've been invaded by lots of people's emotions at the same time. You've never experienced it, so you won't understand. It's the greatest pleasure there is. Here, listen."

He leaned towards me.

"In this life, the proper way of living is to make use of both joy and suffering. They are both merely stimuli that the world presents to us. So by blending them skillfully within you, you can use them in a completely different way. If you want to be steeped in evil, you mustn't forget good. When you see a woman writhing in agony, laughter is unimaginative. When you see a woman writhing in agony, pity her, feel sorry for her, imagine her pain, imagine the parents who raised her even, weep tears of sympathy— while torturing her even more. That moment is just exquisite! Taste everything in the whole world. Even if you should fail at these tasks, taste the emotion that comes with failure. Savor with all your senses the fear of death. When you can do that, you transcend yourself. You can look at this world through different eyes. Straight after I brutally murder someone, the sunrise appears so beautiful, and I look at the smiling face of a child and think how adorable it is. If that child is an orphan, I may help her or I may kill her there and then. Even as I pity her! If gods or fate had personalities and emotions, don't you think this is close to what they would feel? In this world where children and saints die outrageous deaths?"

At this point the man stopped talking. His voice, thick with alcohol, lay heavy and cloying in my ears. As always, he kept on smiling.

"Well, good luck."

13 The first man, Kirita, was forty-two years old and lived in an apartment in Gotanda. His photo showed short hair and a well-tailored suit. He was a broker who acted as a go-between between unlisted companies and the mob. He'd offer to negotiate deals for start-ups who couldn't get financing from the banks. If their business grew, their share price would go up and they'd make a big profit. In that case, the company that took the loan would never know that it came from the mob. All I needed from him was his cell phone, but it's always difficult stealing from a specific target.

After committing the simple notes and the photo to memory, I strolled in front of Kirita's condo. If there'd been a coffee shop nearby I could have watched through the window, but there was nothing like that, and just standing around on a residential street doesn't look natural. When I saw the curtains of his room move, I looked down and walked off. Finding a park some distance away, I sat on a rusty bench. A mother and child were playing silently beside a narrow slide. I stared at the child's head, thinking it was a piece of wood with a hole in it, but he was just wearing a paper bag. They were fooling around, the woman chasing after her fleeing son. I could see the entrance to the condo out of the corner of my eye, but it was too far away to see people clearly.

After about four hours a man in a cream coat with a shoulder bag walked out and headed off in the opposite direction. I couldn't see his face but I hurried after him, thinking it might be Kirita. He was hunched over like a shrimp, his unusually long fingers splayed. Just as I reached the entrance, the automatic door opened again and another man came out. A black coat, carrying a black satchel. *That's him*, I thought, taken by surprise. I lowered my head and pretended to be hunting in my pockets for cigarettes. Taking his phone without him realizing it, so that he thought he'd lost it, seemed an impossible demand. I tailed him, keeping my distance.

He went to a drug-store and then to the station, where he met up with a fat man in a café. His wallet was in the left inside pocket of his suit, but he kept his cell phone in his satchel. It looked like it would be hard to steal it while he was inside, so I waited for him to leave. I thought about lifting it on the train, but when he came out and said good-bye to the fat man he got into a taxi. I took the next cab and told the driver to follow the car in front of us. The driver was still young, so I kept having to give him exact instructions, like to stay in a different lane and keep another car between us.

Kirita got out in Akasaka and went into a basement bar. The interior was large, with a stage for performers, and incredibly crowded and noisy. I found a seat at the counter, thinking that this might be my chance. I ordered a weak cocktail and rested my arms on the wooden surface, which had darkened with age.

An hour or more passed. As Kirita grew more intoxicated, his voice became louder and his gestures more exaggerated. He was laughing, his reptilian mouth open wide. The other guy was young, maybe a student. Papers were spread out on the table but Kirita barely glanced at them.

He took his cell phone out of his bag, made a call, and then replaced the phone in the satchel on the floor. I was hoping he would put it in his jacket, but no such luck. Seeing how drunk he was, if I took his phone today he would easily believe that he'd lost it, and I didn't know when I'd get another opportunity like this. Plus his was the earliest of the deadlines Kizaki had given me. When the waitress approached his table I stood up.

The toilets were on his other side, away from me. I headed towards them, adjusting my pace to that of the waitress. She put fresh glasses on his table, and just as she bowed and turned to leave I tripped her, as if by accident. She tumbled over and the glasses on her tray shattered spectacularly. I pretended to lose my balance and fell down too, but while everyone turned at the loud noise they were all looking at the waitress lying on the floor in her short skirt. When I checked on Kirita, he was facing her in surprise and touching his shoulder, which was slightly damp. Still crouching, I used my coat like a cape to cover his bag. I slipped my left hand through the hole in my pocket, and was able to open the zipper. The young man stood up and started to say something to Kirita. As the waitress struggled to her feet she tugged at her skirt, which had ridden up, and opened her mouth to apologize. With the bag completely concealed under my jacket, no one could see anything. I put my left hand inside, hunted quickly for the phone, hooked my finger through the strap and slid it into my sleeve. Kirita started to rise to help the waitress. Pulling my hand out of the satchel, I braced my legs to stand. Just as I felt the warmth escaping from my throat, the phone in my sleeve shrilled loudly.

I froze for a second, unable to move. As the ringing continued, Kirita began to turn away from the woman toward the noise. I dropped the phone back in the bag and concentrated on doing up the zip. The sound grew muffled but he didn't seem to notice. The waitress said sorry to both Kirita and me. Heart pounding, I stood up and apologized as well. Kirita wasn't looking at me, though. He opened the satchel and answered the phone. I thought about making my exit, but it seemed important to hear his conversation, so I helped the waitress pick up the glass. Kirita didn't speak, but I managed to catch a glimpse of the notes he made: Thursday, 7, Shibuya, Daijingu. I nodded again and paid my bill. Now that he'd seen my face up close, shadowing him would be tricky.

I TOOK A cab back to my apartment, asking the driver if I could smoke. He said he didn't mind because he was finishing up for the day and opened the window a fraction. I lit up and watched the neon lights flowing past in the busy streets. I just couldn't relax. Kizaki's face appeared in front of me, then Ishikawa's, then Saeko's. I wondered what she would say if she saw me now. I was going down in the world, being manipulated, dancing to Kizaki's tune, but still I thought she probably wouldn't despise me. Knowing her, she'd be more likely to laugh as she undressed, saying maybe we'll die soon, and come down here with me.

When I got home the boy was asleep on the floor outside my front door. This time he was wearing long trousers, but his gray sweatshirt was thin. Looking at his arms and legs, I felt once more that his life had been determined at birth. In his downtrodden situation he just did the best he could and kept on going. I prodded him lightly with my foot, thinking he'd die of cold, and he opened his eyes. He scowled at me for a second, maybe because I'd kicked him. But before I could say anything he quietly asked me to let him stay for the night.

"Nothing doing. Go home."

"Why not?"

The boy's breath came out in faint white puffs.

"Because your mom will come looking for you and the cops will get involved."

"That's not going to happen."

"No?"

"She wants to get rid of me."

He stood up, brushing sand and grime from the palms of his hands. His skin was dirty and the soles of his shoes were almost worn through. I was about to let him in, but then realized that I didn't have a kettle or plates or anything to eat. We'd have to go to a convenience store. When I walked off, the boy came with me.

"He's there all the time now and I'm in the way."

"Did he tell you that?"

"He's always telling me, because he wants to do it with Mom all the time."

In the distance I heard the sound of a car accelerating.

"He's jealous about Mom. Because they're always at it, I have to be out all day. And when they're finished he gets drunk and hits me."

I put my hand on his shoulder.

"This guy. Does he know what your mother. . . ?"

"He knows. He makes her do it but he still gets jealous."

My throat felt tight.

"You want to get out?"

"Yeah."

There was a strange gleam in his eyes.

"I'd run away, but I'm just a kid and I'd get caught. And then I'd get bawled out, and if he was there he'd beat me up."

"Well, you can't stay here. . . ."

"Why not?"

I took my hand off his shoulder. Probably I picked the wrong time to do it.

"My job's risky. I don't know when I might get killed. You don't need to get mixed up with any more adults who've messed up their lives."

"But. . . ."

"What about a children's home?"

I looked at his face. He seemed to be thinking seriously.

"Could I get into one?"

"If you go through the formalities. But when it comes down to it you don't really want to be away from your mom, do you?"

"I'm not a baby."

He looked up at me. His wide defiant eyes, like two laser beams, reminded me of myself a long time ago.

"I'll talk to her. And from now on I'll leave my room unlocked, so if it's cold you can go in whenever you like."

With that, we went into the convenience store and bought hot tea, milk and a lunch box full of fried food.

14

My second target was a twenty-eight-year-old man who lived in a seven-story apartment building. I didn't know what he did for a living, but judging from his dress and demeanor he wasn't exactly a big player in the underworld. His condo was also in a residential area, so I couldn't just loiter out on the street. I watched the passers-by through the windows of a nearby café. He was bound to go this way to get to the station. He didn't have a car or a bike. I waited for a couple hours, but he didn't appear. I left the coffee shop, ambled along the road in front of his condo and then returned to my post.

It was noon on the second day of my stake-out when he came out of the building. I'd come by taxi and waited for a while, but there was no sign of him. I'd just placed my order in the café when I saw him walking towards me. I left the shop and followed him. He went to the station, through the turnstile and onto the platform. If they were going to leave his lighter and hairs next to a dead body, that meant he must have a record. It was hard to believe, though—he looked even more baby-faced and meek than he did in his photo.

Fortunately the train was crowded. I stood right behind him, thinking this would be the best place. His black hair was lightly styled with wax. There were no loose hairs on his neck or shoulders, so I'd have to pluck them out directly. The carriage was overheated and he was sweating. As the train came to a stop he moved closer to the passenger in front as though he was planning to get off, and I pressed myself right up against his back. Attached roughly to the tips of my forefinger and middle finger were pieces of a nail file I'd found at home. The doors opened, letting in the cold air. When he took a step forward I pretended to lose my balance. Raising my hand as though clutching at air, I pinched a few strands of hair between my fingers and pulled. I felt a slight tug as they came out. He turned involuntarily, but I slipped past so that I was in front of him. Now all I needed was his lighter.

He seemed to be heading towards the stairs, but then he suddenly changed direction. I realized he was going to the smoking area on the platform for the Yamanote line. He took out his cigarettes and hunted for his lighter. My first reaction was that I'd be in trouble if he'd lost it, but then I had a brainwave. Putting on my gloves, I wiped my own cheap disposable lighter several times inside my jacket. Then I stood right beside him and lit up. He was still searching, and just as he was about to give up I silently handed him mine. He nodded his thanks and used it to light his cigarette. I thought the fingerprints might not look natural, so when he returned the lighter I fumbled it and it fell to the ground. He picked it up for me. This time I took it, and the job was finished. I boarded the next train and got out of there.

. . .

I WENT TO a hairdresser's to get my hair cut and dyed brown. Then I put on a pair of glasses with fake lenses. The day I met Kirita I had been wearing my usual black coat, so I changed my image with a white down jacket and jeans. At six in the evening I headed for Shibuya. I was sure I'd find him there, in a bar called Daijingu. Since he'd only seen me for a second he probably wouldn't remember me, but just on the off-chance I needed a disguise.

I spotted him from the cab when we stopped at a red light in front of the Seibu department store in Shibuya. He was in the same black coat as before, carrying the same satchel. I got out of the car and followed him. The narrow street was overflowing with people and every time he paused I moved closer. Maybe I could take it before he reached the bar. He stopped at a red light. I was standing right behind him, but for some reason the woman beside me was staring at him, so I couldn't do anything. The lights turned green and I stayed on his heels through the dense crowd.

Just as I'd made up my mind to do it at the next intersection, Kirita turned round abruptly. I tensed up, but he hadn't spotted me. I looked away as he passed. After giving him a head start, I tailed him again. He went into a Parco store. Inside he glanced around and then headed for the escalator. Because people are standing at different heights, escalators are perfect for stealing things from their bags. I stood behind him as we went up, psyched myself up for it. There were mirrors along the side so I waited for a gap. The man behind me was chatting to the woman below him, not looking in my direction. I figured this was the ideal place and the ideal time. I felt the warmth inside me, was aware of a pleasant numbness in my arms. As soon as his head was in the dead space between two mirrors, I grabbed the bottom of his satchel with my left hand so that it wouldn't shake and undid the zip with my right. Then I pulled out his cell phone and hid it in my sleeve, closed the zip again and let go of the bag. When he moved on to the next up escalator I veered off to the left, watching him out of the corner of my eye. I looked for the stairs on that floor and went down. My body went limp and a tremor passed through me as I transferred the phone to my pocket.

Back out on the busy Shibuya streets I snuck my hand into the pocket of an expensively dressed man walking towards me, hid his wallet in my sleeve. The afterimage of the light reflecting off his tie pin remained as a green spot in my eye. I took a cab and checked what was in the wallet. It held 120,000 yen, several credit cards and a bunch of business cards handed out by women from hostess bars. The confined spaces of taxis, isolated from the city and the people, always gave me the feeling that I could escape.

I STAYED IN the car and headed for Ebisu. The apartment building I'd been directed to was fairly new and clean. Once I put these in the mailbox for room 702, two of my tasks would be finished. As instructed, I opened it, removed the white envelope inside and replaced it with the bag containing the cell phone, lighter and hair. I thought about watching from a distance to see who came to collect it, but instead I caught another cab and opened the envelope. This would be the photo of the guy I had to steal the documents from, plus basic information like his address. As I took out the picture I felt uneasy. A man in his forties, thinning hair, sunken eyes and hollow cheeks. Looking at his face, I could tell he wasn't someone you wanted to mess with. In the past it was uncanny how often my hunches had turned out to be correct. I wanted a smoke to calm my nerves, but the driver said I couldn't, so I got out.

Lighting a cigarette, I walked along an unfamiliar street through a housing estate with rows of elderly apartment buildings and not many streetlights. Suddenly my cell phone rang and I looked around foolishly. The only people who knew this number were Saeko and Ishikawa. The caller ID was blocked and when I answered it, it was a man I didn't know.

"That was quick, only one left. You got the envelope from the mailbox?"

His voice was unpleasantly high and harsh.

"Who is this?"

"I think you can guess. The last guy, Yonezawa, will be in Shinjuku at eight o'clock tomorrow night. Grab it then."

"What if I can't?"

"You've got till next Tuesday. Five days left. But thanks to you, my job has gotten a whole lot easier. I hear that if you don't succeed you're going to die. Don't think about doing a runner, though."

A young blonde walking her dog was looking at me strangely.

"Is Kizaki with you?"

"Mr. Kizaki? No. I don't know where he is."

"What's he really after?"

The man on the other end sighed wearily.

"I don't mean just the papers and the lighter," I said.

"That's none of your business."

Behind him I could hear a woman's faint laughter. The background noise gradually grew louder and then the line went dead. The woman was still watching me as her plump pet sniffed urgently at a telephone pole. When I stared back, she spoke to the dog and dragged him away. The area was dark. Perhaps she hadn't been looking at me at all, but at something just behind me.

15

In his photo Yonezawa was wearing a scruffy black coat, but his condo was big enough to have a reception desk and getting inside wouldn't be easy. I didn't know what he did for a living, but if he walked around with a gun in his pocket he was probably no saint. Looking at the deep-set eyes in his picture I felt that murder or something similar was lurking behind them.

I hired a car and parked in a place where I could keep an eye on the entrance to his building, but not too close.

Though there was a risk the cops might ask what I was doing there, a car is definitely best for surveillance. I expected to see a taxi pull up outside his apartment, but when he came out he left on foot. He walked with a bounce, as though he was dragging his feet slightly. He looked idly around, glared at some children coming towards him.

I got out of the car and tailed him, keeping a safe distance. He was clearly a man who didn't like spending money. If he was living in a place like this, I figured he must really feel he was in danger. In the station he took a long time buying his ticket. After casting his eye over the people around him, he fixed his gaze on a woman in a skimpy outfit, staring at her intently. I shifted further away. It didn't look like I'd be able to get close to him until we got on the train.

When he reached the platform, Yonezawa scratched his neck several times and checked out a woman in a coat standing near him. His hair was oddly slicked down and his cheeks were dotted with freckles that hadn't shown up in the photo. His shoes were filthy. When the train arrived it was hardly crowded at all. I opened my newspaper, still keeping a good distance from him. Yonezawa didn't sit, but stood in a corner with a vacant look on his face.

His wallet was jammed tightly in his right front pocket, but he wasn't carrying a bag and I couldn't tell where the envelope was. Probably in his inside coat pocket, I thought, but the chances of taking it now looked slim. Gradually, however, the train started to fill up, and I mentally prepared myself. I got up, threaded my way through the passengers and stood in front of the door.

At Ikebukuro a whole lot of people got off, but even more got on, so that it was hard to move inside the carriage. An announcement over the loudspeaker told us that we were approaching Shinjuku. Then the doors opened and the crowd started to move. I focused on edging closer to Yonezawa in the crush. When my body was right up against his I unbuttoned his coat and slipped my hand inside. His breath felt unpleasant against my cheek. My fingertips felt something shaped like an envelope and I thought I could take it, but when I extended my fingers I realized that the inner pocket was closed up. Not with a button or a zip, but actually sewn shut. With a dull pain in my heart I quickly withdrew my hand. Merging with the river of people boarding, I shoved close to him again and fastened his coat once more. The crowd continued to heave violently.

Yonezawa exited onto the platform, and just before the doors closed I got off, too. My pulse was racing. It was impossible to switch the envelope sewn into his pocket with the one I had. If I cut the stitches to steal it, there was no way he wouldn't notice for two days. I followed him slowly, but I didn't have a clue what I should do next. Maybe I could somehow replace his whole jacket with a different one, but I'd never be able to buy a coat that matched his shabby old thing. Even if I could find something similar, it would be hard to reproduce exactly the same worn patches. It was inconceivable that someone as highly-strung as he was wouldn't notice the difference.

Yonezawa took the east exit towards Kabukicho. His body swung as he walked, his eyes scanning the crowd. He tripped and lost his balance, then scowled at a passing woman for a few seconds before going into a gray building. I thought about going to see Kizaki, but I didn't know where to find him. Remembering the condo in Ebisu, I decided to visit room 702. I caught a cab and all the way there my head was filled with images of Ishikawa and Saeko's faces.

When I arrived I took the elevator up and pressed the doorbell of the apartment. After a silence, a man's voice came over the intercom. I told him my name and the door opened. The guy who came out looked at me sullenly and then went back inside. I didn't think it was the same one I'd talked to on the phone yesterday. The room resembled Ishikawa's old office, just a desk and sofa on a gray carpet.

"What do you want?" he asked gruffly.

I stood directly in front of him.

"Yonezawa's got the envelope sewn inside his jacket. It'll be impossible to steal it without him knowing."

"I don't give a shit."

"I want to talk to Kizaki."

"Tough."

He stared at me like I was a real pain in the ass, sat at the desk and turned on the TV. A woman in a bikini ran across the screen as if she were chasing something.

"If I fail, it'll make things harder for you guys too, won't it? Let me talk to Kizaki. If you don't, you could be in deep shit." I paused. "Well, if you won't help me, I'll go."

Still gazing at the screen, the man muttered something and picked up the phone without looking at me. He spoke into it quietly, then took his ear away from the receiver, turned the TV off and sighed. Racing papers and candies were scattered around the desk. He passed me the phone. After a short wait a man I didn't know answered. I told him I wanted to talk to Kizaki and he said I couldn't, but then there was another pause and Kizaki came on. He told me I had five minutes. There was no doubt it was him, but his voice was so low he sounded like a different person.

"Yonezawa's envelope is sewn inside his coat. There's no way I can switch it. Can't I just steal it?"

There was a brief silence and then he laughed.

"Bad luck. What a shame."

"What is?"

"If you can't do it, you die. That's what I promised, isn't it? Though I guess I'll let the woman and her brat go."

"But if I don't succeed, won't that cause trouble for you?"

He laughed again.

"I didn't think you'd be so attached to your life."

He was holding the receiver so close to his mouth that I could almost feel his breath in my ear. His voice crackled.

"And no, it wouldn't bother me too much. Anyway, apparently he'll be going to Shinjuku again three days from now. Try again then. If you can't do it, we'll just have to kill him and snatch the envelope. It would be worth more if we could get it without killing him, but them's the breaks. It's no big deal."

"But. . . ."

"You knew if you failed you'd die. That was our agreement. I never change my mind. Fate shows no mercy. Yours is a cruel life. I've been checking up on you."

I caught my breath.

"Don't think so much. In the course of history billions of people have died. You'll just be one more among them. It's all a game. Don't take life too seriously."

I tried to speak but nothing came out.

"I told you, didn't I? I've got your destiny inside my head. It's addictive. Anyway, you've got four days. It's unfortunate but it can't be helped. People like you nearly always end up like this. Right, listen. It makes no difference to me whether you succeed or fail and die. I never change my mind, so if you fail I will kill you. It's as simple as that. I've got dozens of people like you working for me. You're just one among many. You're just a tiny fraction of all the feelings that pass through me. Things that are trivial to the people at the top of the pyramid are matters of life and death to those beneath them. That's the way the world works. And above all—"

He paused for a second.

"You do not make any demands. Do not ask any questions. Maybe you can't understand me, but that's how it is. Life is unfair. All over the world there are millions of children starving to death as soon as they're born. Dying like flies. That's just how it is."

Kizaki hung up.

I RETURNED TO Shinjuku, to the office building where I'd lost track of Yonezawa. I didn't expect that he'd still be there, and even if he was I probably wouldn't be able to do anything about it. Leaving the busy streets and the hotels behind, I came out in a residential area in the middle of nowhere, with rows and rows of apartment blocks. It was late at night but many of the windows were still lit up. I guess people were still awake because the next day was a holiday. The lights were soft and fuzzy in the darkness.

As I looked up at them, feeling restless, I sensed something unfamiliar in the inside pocket of my coat. I took out a wallet I didn't recognize and a silver Zippo lighter. The wallet contained 79,000 yen, various credit cards, a driver's license and a golf club membership card. My vision contracted. A bloated dog eyed me, then slunk off watch-fully. I saw a man walking towards me wearing a raincoat. *It's not raining*, I thought, and when I looked again there was just a large stain on a wall. It wasn't even shaped like a person.

In a narrow alley off to the left I spotted the lights of a small bar. I tucked the wallet back inside my coat and put the lighter in the basket of a bike lying on its side. The place was tiny, its feebly illuminated sign faded to black. I couldn't read the name.

Inside there were four stools at the counter and two tables. I ordered a whiskey from the seedy bartender, who didn't look at me, and took a seat at a table. An office worker who looked like a regular was passed out drunk, sound asleep with his forehead resting on the bar.

Classical music was flowing out of small speakers and the barman moved absent-mindedly, as though listening to it was his sole purpose in life. A mongrel was tied up beside the counter, sprawled motionless on the floor, only its eyes moving. The man ignored me as he placed a scotch on the rocks on my table. Looking idly around the room, I figured this bar would never be popular.

I soon finished my drink and asked for another. The

barman put a bottle and ice on the table and went back behind the counter. Neither Ishikawa, who used to stop me from drinking too much, nor Saeko, who had urged me to drink more, was there, of course. I began to feel drunk and the glass in front of me seemed to grow dim, and then so did everything else.

There was no one else in the bar apart from the owner, still listening to his music, the unconscious man in the suit, and the dog, which looked bored out of its mind but didn't seem to object to its leash. I thought about my own mortality, about what I had done with my life until now. Reaching out my hands to steal, I had turned my back on everything, rejected community, rejected wholesomeness and light. I had built a wall arround myself and lived by sneaking into the gaps in the darkness of life. Despite that, however, for some reason I felt that I wanted to be here for a little while longer.

The barman was sitting on a chair behind the counter with his eyes closed. I knew nothing about music, so I just watched him as he listened. There were many things I didn't like about my life, but there were also some things I didn't want to lose, people I didn't want to lose. The people I cared about didn't live very long, though, their lives ending in heartbreak. I wondered what my life had meant, thought about it ending, thought about the moment of my death.

The guy in the suit went on sleeping, and the bartender hadn't moved a muscle. If I could, I planned to watch them until I fell asleep myself.

16

When I was young, there was always the tower in the distance.

In dirty lanes lined with row houses and low-rise apartments, every time I looked up I could dimly make it out. Covered in mist, its outline vague, like a spire in some ancient daydream. Solemn, beautiful, exotic, so tall that I couldn't see the top and so far away that no matter how long I walked I'd never reach it.

I would go into a store and slip a rice ball into my little

pocket. Other people's possessions weighed heavy in my hands, like foreign objects. Yet I never felt any guilt or wickedness in these actions. My growing body demanded a lot of food and I didn't see how there could be anything wrong with taking and eating it. Other people's rules were just something they'd invented for themselves. I put that weighty rice ball in my mouth, chewed and swallowed vigorously. Then I stared beyond the lines of power poles, beyond the grubby houses, beyond the trees on the low hill, at the high tower standing in that obscure realm. One day, perhaps, it would speak to me. Scratching my thighs, which poked out of my shorts, I was faintly aware of the stolen property sitting heavy in my stomach.

I heard the laughing cries of a group of children my own age. A boy with long hair was holding a little toy car. It was bought overseas, he shouted in a piercing voice. Operated by a small controller he held in his hand, the sophisticated car sparkled brilliantly as it went racing around.

My heart pounded when I saw it. The boy was boasting about something he hadn't bought himself, that had been given to him. It was revolting. To cure his ugliness, I thought it would be good if he lost his car. I took it. Since the kids didn't even know I was there, it was all too easy to take. For some reason items from other countries always reminded me of the tower.

Alone in an unsealed alley I played quietly with the car, but it wasn't as shiny as it had been before. Something felt wrong and I switched it off, distressed. I placed it further away, turned it on gingerly. When it moved I felt that something still wasn't right. I turned it off again and moved it even further. Finally I threw the car into the muddy river bank. Far, far away, there stood the tower. It remained tall in the distance, silent and shrouded in mist.

It never occurred to me to wonder why there was a tower outside my town. Perhaps I assumed that it had already been there when I was born. The world was fixed and rigid. It was as though time flowed at its own pace, anchoring everything, pushing me from behind, little by little moving me somewhere. When I reached out my hands for other people's things, however, in the tension of the moment I felt I could be set free. I felt I could separate myself just a little from the unbending world.

When I started elementary school, the boy who was chosen as class leader got hold of a glittering watch. "It's my father's," he said, showing it furtively to the people around him. "It even works underwater." The children all stared at this watch that kept going even when submerged. I stole it.

Why did I drop it while everyone was looking at me? My hand had moved swiftly, and by the time it was halfway into my shorts pocket I thought I was home free. But it slipped out and fell with a crash. Everyone looked first at the watch, which had stopped working when it hit the floor, and then at me.

"Thief!" the class leader shouted. "It's broken. That was expensive. Too good for trash like you."

The din in the classroom grew louder. Hands reached out to seize my arms and legs. I was jostled and knocked over. Hearing the cries, the young teacher came over and grabbed my arm. He looked flustered by the children's accusations.

"Say you're sorry!" His voice was also loud. "If you really took it, say you're sorry!"

Looking back on it now, perhaps this was a kind of liberation, because this was the first time my actions had been exposed to the outside world, with the exception of the tower. I felt a sense of freedom that I'd never experienced before. Overpowered, in the midst of my disgrace, I felt pleasure seeping through me. If you can't stop the light from shining in your eyes, it's best to head back down in the opposite direction.

I didn't hide my smirk, I didn't resist, I just lay there on the floor as they held me down. Through the classroom window I could see the tower. *Perhaps now it will tell me something*, I thought. Because it had been standing there for such a long, long time. But it still just stood there, beautiful and remote, neither accepting nor rejecting me as I took pleasure in my humiliation. I closed my eyes.

I decided I would keep on stealing until I could no longer see the tower. Sinking lower and lower, deeper and deeper into the shadows. The more I stole, I believed, the further I would move away from the tower. Before long the tension of stealing became more and more attractive. The strain as my fingers touched other people's things and the reassuring warmth that followed. It was the act of denying all values, trampling all ties. Stealing stuff I needed, stealing stuff I didn't need, throwing away what I didn't need after I stole it. The thrill that vanquishes the strange feeling that ran down to the tips of my fingers when my hands reached into that forbidden zone. I don't know whether it was because I crossed a certain line or simply because I was growing older, but without my realizing it the tower had vanished.

17

When I called the boy's mother she said that she wanted to go to a hotel, so I took a taxi. We met in the middle of the day in front of a pachinko parlor, walked through the hotel district and picked one at random. As soon as we got to the room she started to undress, saying she knew that I'd call her again. I started to say something about the boy, but got into bed with her instead, partly because it would be hard to talk to her if I made her mad, but also because I had the wretched feeling that I was going to die soon and I wanted to touch a woman one last time. She climbed on top of me and, thanks to her tablets, just kept on coming, digging in her fingernails.

Still naked, she got out of bed and opened the curtains a crack. Scratching her cheek, she told me that they'd built a new shopping mall over the road. She seemed to want to show it to me. Her clothes lay on the floor like a flattened corpse. A thin ray of sunlight peeped through the curtains. I raised myself slightly in the bed.

"By the way," I started, unsure if this was the right time or not. "How would you feel about giving up the boy?"

Her face froze for a second as she turned.

"To you?"

For some reason she smiled as she said this.

"No, a children's home."

"Could I?"

I thought she'd be angry, but she closed the curtains and came back to the bed.

"Yes, you could. You'd need to do some paperwork."

"Yuck," she said suddenly, turning away and lighting a cigarette.

I guessed it was the probably the paperwork she was talking about.

"I've got to disappear for a while. I won't be able to see him again. It would be better if he didn't live with you. If he wasn't there, things would go more smoothly with your man, wouldn't they? And if you put him in a home I'll give you five hundred thousand yen. How about that?"

"What?"

Slowly she turned to face me. Like her lips, her eyes were faintly moist, with a sad gleam. I realized that I was getting turned on again and looked away.

"My boyfriend, he's been punching him lately. He probably won't kill him, but it's still abuse, isn't it? You see it on the news. I'd hate it if that happened. The cops would come, wouldn't they? Did you mean it?"

"I've got plenty of money. It's not that much to me. If you get in touch with the Child Guidance Center they'll look after him. If they can't, contact this foster home. You can trust them. But if you just take the money and don't put him in care without a damn good reason, there'll be trouble. I'm going away but I'll be asking my friends to keep an eye on you. They're yakuza. Get it?"

I don't know if she was listening or not, but suddenly she licked my lips.

"If my parents were around I could leave him with them, but they're not. I've been wondering what to do. You're right, we could put him in one of those places. I hadn't thought of that. So all I have to do is call them, right? Hey, with that much I could go on a trip!"

She tucked the paper I'd given her into her purse. I took the money from my jacket, which I'd tossed in a heap on the floor.

"You're paying me now?" she asked, but immediately stowed it in her bag.

One eye blinked tightly several times.

"You're great. Really awesome. I'm so happy! Now, what'll I buy with this? I mean, what good are kids, anyway? Know what I mean? They're only cute for the first couple of months, eh?"

When I got out of the cab in front of my apartment, the boy was standing there. In his hands he held an open can of Coke and a can of coffee, the brand I usually drink. He passed it to me wordlessly, so I opened it there and then. He looked at my dyed hair but didn't comment. The coffee was almost cold.

I went inside briefly and when I came out again he followed me. A car sped by, startling him, and he grabbed the hem of my coat. It was low-slung, with mindless music blaring out at full volume. Coming towards us was a little girl clutching her father's jacket in the same way. The boy and I passed by them without a word. The man said something to his daughter and she answered sulkily.

We ambled along the side of a small river well outside the city. The banks were well tended but the water was murky, with plastic bottles and other trash floating in it. The kid looked like he wanted to say something but kept quiet, hesitant. I lit a cigarette and gazed out over the sluggish river.

"I talked to her. You're sure about going into a home, right? That would mean you'd be getting out of there."

"Yeah."

His voice was a bit stronger than before. I passed him a slip of paper.

"If your mom tries to keep you at home and you still don't like it, call this number. This agency will take care of everything."

He stared at the number like he was trying to memorize it.

"You can still start over. You can do whatever you want. Forget about stealing and shoplifting."

"Why?"

He was gazing up at me.

"You'll never find a place in society."

"But. . . ."

"Shut up. Just forget it."

My lifestyle certainly didn't qualify me to be giving advice to children. I held out a small box.

"I'm giving you this."

"What is it?"

"In the end I didn't need it. Open it when you need strength, or when you're in real trouble. Like you're done for and might as well die. Pretty cool, eh?"

"But what if someone takes it away, too?"

"Okay, let's bury it somewhere."

I spotted a hiking trail and we headed up the dirt-colored road. Partway along we came across a stone statue of a woman laughing crazily. I used my empty can and my hands to dig a deep hole in the earth behind it. The inscription on the plinth was almost entirely worn away, but it seemed to be some kind of memorial. I didn't think they'd be doing roadwork here, so no one was likely to dig the box up.

"If you end up not needing it," I told the boy, "give it to a kid like you."

We continued walking in silence. The sun was gradually sinking and the air grew chilly. When we came out into a clearing, I found a tennis ball someone had dropped. I picked it up casually and brushed off the dirt with my hands. On the other side of a bench we could see a boy playing catch with his father. He was about the same age as my kid, but his throw was weak and clumsy. Every time he threw, his dad said something to him. A digital camera and portable game console, probably theirs, were lying on the bench.

"Are you any good at throwing a ball?"

"Dunno."

"I bet you're better than that useless brat."

I threw the ball a long way away. He hesitated for a second and then ran to fetch it. The others realized we were there and turned to look at us. The boy collected the ball and hurled it back at me. I felt it sting my fingers as I caught it. I threw it back even harder, but he caught it with two hands and returned it more powerfully than the first time. When he saw me fumble it he laughed. The father and son were watching us, and after a couple of minutes I worked out that it must be their ball. I thanked them like a regular person, tossed it back to them underarm. The boy ran back to me, a little out of breath.

"Listen," I told him. "I've got to go on a long trip, so I won't be able to see you any more. But don't waste your life. Even if there's times when you're miserable, you'll always have the last laugh."

He nodded. He never did hold my hand, but as we walked home he gripped the edge of my coat again.

"First, buy some clothes. Some decent clothes."

18

Wearing a black coat, I stood at the edge of the platform and watched Yonezawa.

I checked that the knife was still in my pocket and pretended to be reading a newspaper. He scowled at some laughing children. When a woman walked by he followed her with his eyes. Finally he looked down and started to walk. He bumped into a businessman but kept going without an apology. When the train arrived I got into the same carriage as him. It was full, though not so full that people were jammed together. I positioned myself a little away from him, continuing to read my paper. He leaned against the doors of the swaying train, his arms hanging loosely by his sides.

At Ikebukuro a lot of people got off but even more got on. A group of high school girls in sportswear piled on at the last minute and the carriage grew crowded. Maybe now, I thought, folding my paper and moving closer to Yonezawa. But he was moving slowly towards the girls, frowning and clicking his tongue in disapproval. He stood out like a sore thumb as he forced his way through the packed car. When he got close to the girls, he stopped and glared at them. Didn't open his mouth, didn't touch them, just stood next to them, staring.

I thought that if I moved he'd see me, so I waited till the next station. Not many passengers got on or off. I inched closer to Yonezawa until I was right behind him. One of the hemmed-in high school girls was squirming in discomfort. I pinched the material on the left side of his coat between my fingers. His body jerked as the girl tried to put her bag up as a barrier between herself and him. At that moment I slowly cut his jacket from top to bottom. The opening didn't reach his inside pocket, however. I exhaled softly. The air in the carriage was thick and I was getting hot.

He looked at the schoolbag between them and seemed to give up, contenting himself with scowling. He started touching his collar. It could only be a matter of seconds before he looked down and spotted the slit. Holding my breath, which had been quickening, I stretched out my left foot and kicked one of the girls lightly on the leg. She jumped, yelped and turned slowly to look at Yonezawa. His skinny frame trembled in surprise and I slid the knife back into the side of his coat. Lifting the fabric with my fingers, I began to cut his inside pocket, slicing it little by little with the tip of the blade. I spread my fingers, holding the knife between with my thumb and index finger and pinching the envelope between my middle and ring fingers. A shiver ran from my fingers up to my shoulder. Ignoring my nervousness, I pulled it out. I could see out of the corner of my eye that the envelope was quite different from the dummy I was to replace it with. *Worse and worse*, I thought, with a sinking feeling. The girl turned away again, perhaps out of fear, and before I knew it the train arrived at Shinjuku.

Watching Yonezawa as he walked ahead of me on the platform, I took out the envelope. The fake was green and white, but this was an ordinary brown one. My hands were shaking slightly, but when I held it up to the light I could see another envelope inside. I opened the brown envelope and removed the second, which was green and white with a company name printed on it, just like the dummy. I sighed with relief. Overall, however, it was battered and discolored. The difference between it and the dummy, still clean and new, was obvious. Massive buildings loomed all round the platform. Baffled, head aching, I trailed after Yonezawa. He went out the east exit and joined the crowds outside. When he spied a group of loudly dressed women, he stopped. Then he turned round and our eyes almost met. I went back into the station, bought a can of coffee from a kiosk and leaned against the glass by the entrance, my back to the street. After a few deep breaths I opened my cell phone and punched in Yonezawa's number, which I had written on a piece of paper. Sweat trickled down my jaw.

I could see him in the distance in the square outside

Alta. He seemed to be talking to himself, because the people around him were staring in astonishment. He looked around, pawing at the side of his jacket. Soon he noticed the ringing and stuck his hand in his pocket. When he answered the phone he was panting.

"Yonezawa?" I said quietly.

He didn't reply.

"I said, is that Yonezawa? Answer me."

"Who is this?"

"Have you lost an envelope?"

He snarled something unintelligible. With his phone still clamped to his ear he started walking in my direction, then stopped and studied the people in the square. I wasn't keen on doing business up close with a man who carried a gun.

"You can look as much as you like. I'm nowhere nearby. I'm watching you from a building with binoculars."

"Who are you?"

"That's not important."

He was getting closer to me. I stepped back from the glass, which was steaming up. A man who I guessed was a plain-clothes detective crossed swiftly in front of me.

"You know it's not normal to walk around with things

sewn inside your coat. Some people asked me to get my hands on this. But they're not exactly guys I can trust to pay me, so I've got a better idea. I heard I could turn this into cash. I'm guessing you need it, right? I don't know why such an uninteresting envelope is so important. If you want it back, you'll answer my questions."

"Are you with the company? Or one of Yada's?"

"I don't have to tell you."

"I'm going to kill you."

Several people were looking at him as he paced the area, still dragging one leg slightly. I went into the station and through into the department store next door.

"Answer the questions."

"Shit. I knew it."

"What?"

"I just knew someone was after me. Motherfuckers! This is exactly why I haven't liked going out."

"If you're just going to talk crap, I'll throw it away."

That shut him up.

I went into the toilets and locked myself in a cubicle.

"First, tell me what's in the envelope."

"No fucking way."

"Why not?"

"They'll kill me. Give it back. Please!"

"I'll burn it."

Again he said something I couldn't make out.

"I'm begging you, goddammit. Give it back!"

"It's a bit damp now."

"Huh?"

"I spilled some coffee. If you don't talk to me soon, the papers inside will be ruined."

I dribbled some coffee into my hand and rubbed it very lightly over the surface of the envelope.

"Stop!"

"Aw, it's all dirty now. This is fun."

"All right! I'll pay you."

"Now I'm folding it."

"Listen! It's no use to you. There are channels you have to go through. You won't even be able to do anything with it. I'll pay you. Three hundred thousand yen."

"It's falling to bits."

"Okay, five hundred thousand. That's all I have. I bet that's more than they're giving you."

I crushed the corners of the envelope and compared the dummy with the original. Now the fake was even grubbier than the real one. If you looked closely the seal in the center was at a slightly different angle, but it was in almost exactly the same place.

"All right, I guess I'll have to take your offer. I could use the money just now."

"You're an asshole."

"If you're going to talk like that I really will throw it away."

It was probably already safe to hand it over, but if I made it too easy he might get suspicious about the envelope. I left the toilets and walked past several people. Returning to the station, I climbed the steps to the east entrance.

"Go and get the money from the bank. Then put it in one of the coin lockers in front of the ticket gate for the Yamanouchi line at the east entrance. There's a vending machine next to the kiosk. Put the key where you take out the cans, on the right side. I don't know why, but there are lots of plain-clothes cops around today. Don't do anything stupid."

"Cops?"

"It doesn't matter. Don't even think about watching to see who comes to open the locker. Go straight back to the square and stand somewhere I can see you. I'm watching you. When I know that you're back outside, I'll put the envelope in the same locker and the key back in the same place. Easy."

"How do I know I can trust you? We should make the exchange face to face."

"You don't have a choice."

I hung up. When I went out the east exit I could see Yonezawa in the distance, still clutching his cell phone. He walked off and I followed him with my eyes, keeping a wide gap between us. He went into a bank.

I changed direction and lit a cigarette in the smoking area outside Alta, thinking that it had been a long time since my last one. When I looked up a news flash was being shown on the big screen. A politician had been shot while he was making a speech on the west side of Shinjuku Station. The people on the street were panicking, and the announcer was speaking as gravely as if he'd been shot himself.

Yonezawa came back from the bank and crossed the street at the crosswalk, heading toward the east entrance of the station, but when he saw all the people standing there he turned around and looked up at the screen, not moving. I averted my gaze and kept on smoking. I waited until he started walking again and followed him, keeping well back.

He opened the coin locker and put something inside, then bought a drink from the vending machine. Seeing that he was scanning his surroundings, I went outside again. It was some time before he appeared at the exit again. He stood in the middle of the square and looked around. I looped back to the station and phoned him. After telling him to come to collect the envelope in ten minutes, I hung up. A tall man who looked like a cop passed right beside me with a cell phone in his hand. He disappeared into the crush, shouting.

When I took the key from the vending machine and opened the locker, a bank envelope was inside. I checked it and there was no doubt it held money. I replaced it with the dummy, bought a coffee from the machine and put the key inside as I took out the can.

Suddenly my strength deserted me and I wanted to sit down right where I was, but I had to keep watch until he collected the envelope. Unless he took it without realizing that the papers had been stolen—in other words, unless he thought the fake was the real thing—this whole exchange was pointless. I kept an eye out, staying well back and hiding in the crowd, until I saw Yonezawa. He opened the locker and inspected the envelope. My heart beat faster, but he put it in his pocket without a second glance. I phoned him.

"Did you get it?"

He didn't answer straight away.

"Are you there?"

"It's filthy. A total mess."

I figured that so far he hadn't worked it out.

"It's your own fault. I always do what I say I'm going to. I could have kept it and done a runner, but that sounds like asking for trouble. In fact I'm doing you a favor. You should be grateful."

"One day I'll find you and kill you."

"Try it."

I ended the call and my body went limp. I was dying for a smoke but I realized that several people had turned to look at something behind me. Yonezawa had seized a young man's hand in front of the lockers. The youth, who was holding a cell phone, was untidy and toting a large bag, as though he was traveling by himself.

I could have made my escape, but I thought of Yonezawa roaming around with a gun. I rang him right away, moving nearer. At that instant, however, he seemed to look straight at me, even though we were still a long way apart. I turned away but I could sense him drawing closer. My pulse began to race. I thought about cutting the call, but if the noise stopped just as I was fiddling with my phone it would be a dead giveaway that I was the one on the other end.

I slipped the phone into my pocket, still ringing, and faded back into the crowd. Every time I looked around his eyes met mine. Out of the corner of my eye I could see him clawing his way through the throng like a madman. Just as I climbed the stairs, acting casual and thinking that it would be worse if I ran, he reached my side and grabbed my arm. When I felt his fingers, I gasped. My throat went dry.

"It's you?"

"Huh?"

He was breathing heavily.

"Where's the money?"

I assumed a puzzled expression, but my heart was beating faster than ever.

"The envelope was there, but that was mine in the first place. Give me the money, quickly! And don't make a fuss."

He pressed against me and jabbed something into my gut. I knew without looking that it was a gun. The face that had made such an unpleasant impression on me when I first saw it in the photo was right there in front of me. I had a brief image of Kizaki, and it felt like Ishikawa and Saeko were watching me from nearby.

"Stop it, please."

"I've seen you somewhere. I'm sure of it. I know it's you. It must be."

A few heads started to turn in our direction but no one was paying us any particular attention. Yonezawa's phone kept on ringing like some kind of rite. His eyes bulged and he was sweating profusely. I tried to remain calm, but in those circumstances it would have been unnatural not to be shocked.

"I'm sorry if I've done something."

"Have I got it wrong? Fuck. I'll kill that guy. Where is he? No, it's got to be you. If it's not you I'm fucked."

He was spraying flecks of saliva as he spoke. He started searching the pockets of my coat. I wondered if I should admit it was me and return the money, but considering his deranged state and the possibility that he might find the real envelope, it seemed too dangerous. In spite of the risk of being shot, I thought about trying to escape. At that instant, however, someone caught him by the arm.

"You can't get away from Mr. Yada," said the stranger. "But you made it a fair way. You're Yonezawa. Found you at last."

Yonezawa suddenly punched him, spun around and sprinted off through the curious crowd. I had no idea what was going on and I thought that fleeing was my only option as well, but the guy had already taken hold of my arm. Why wasn't he going after Yonezawa? Why had he captured me? I couldn't move. Just as I was thinking that I was done for, he squeezed my arm even tighter and showed his yellow teeth.

"You're amazing. You really switched it. I was watching the whole time. Mr. Kizaki's orders. The situation has changed, so if you'd failed I would have had to kill Yonezawa straight away and get the papers. I didn't know how you were going to do it. I thought you were about to take off and I almost killed you too. Maybe it would've been better if I had, because that would've created a disturbance and given us some cover for the hit over at the west gate."

THE MAN AND I got in a car. Once inside he took off a light bulletproof vest. He laughed a lot, saying over and over that I was going to be a good addition to Kizaki's gang. One of his ears was missing. Putting a dirty arm round my shoulders, he suggested we go out for a drink sometime.

My cell phone rang. It was Kizaki, of course.

"Have you given him the papers?"

"Not yet."

"You're cautious. That's excellent."

Kizaki laughed, but I still hadn't come to terms with the new situation.

"Because I told you to hand the envelope directly to me. But it's fine, you can give it to him."

I did as instructed.

"To start with, come over here. Get Maejima to bring you."

He hung up and I exhaled. There was no way I wanted to become partners with the guys who murdered Ishikawa. In my inside pocket I still had the knife I'd used to cut

Yonezawa's coat. *It wouldn't be a bad thing if I killed Kizaki with it*, I thought. Obviously I'd die immediately afterwards, though. In that moment I was seized by the conviction that I didn't want that to happen. I didn't know what was holding me back, but the fact that I was trying not to screw up meant I was still clinging to something in this world. For the time being, I turned over in my head ways I could politely refuse to join them.

When we reached the parking lot the man called Maejima let me out of the car first. His cell phone against his one ear, he told me to go to the end of the alley between the buildings and through the door. Then he returned to his cell phone conversation.

The space between the two office blocks was too narrow to be called a street, barely wide enough for two people to pass. There were no signs and I couldn't tell what kind of companies the buildings housed. It felt ominous, but I had no choice but to go in to see Kizaki.

The passage was claustrophobic and smelled of mold. Someone was walking towards me from the other end. I started to turn back, thinking what a tight squeeze it would be, but Maejima was approaching from behind. He looked much bigger than he had before. I turned forward again, wondering why he seemed to have grown. At that moment someone opened an umbrella right in my face, and just as it hit me I felt a fierce heat in my belly. My strength vanished and I collapsed. *It's hot but it doesn't hurt*, I thought, and then I was gripped with a violent pain as though a hand was crushing my insides. My breath stopped and my body shook. I retched but nothing came out. The pain spread to my chest and next, for reasons I didn't understand, to my arms. My vision flickered and I realized that, like it or not, I'd received a fatal blow. Dark blood was forming a pool on the concrete. I saw a pair of shoes in front of me. I tried to look up but couldn't move.

"Hard luck."

It was Kizaki's voice.

"Even though you did everything perfectly, this is what happens. And you don't know why, do you?"

Someone took hold of my coat and casually pulled it off. I was rolled over and I couldn't breathe. The world went black. When I came to I was still in pain.

"Whether you succeeded or whether you failed, I'd already decided that you were going to die in this spot. One reason is that I need a corpse here. It's a bit early, but an hour from now everything will be clear."

He seemed to be smiling.

"It's a shame you won't be around to see how interesting things are going to become from now on. Yes, things are going to get very interesting in this country. The system, with all its megalomaniacs, is really going to change. Dramatically. It's going to have a huge impact on the ordinary people, as well. The world will boil. But still. . . ."

He peered at my face. His eyes were mere slits behind his sunglasses.

"Even that bores me." He laughed out loud. "It's all hell. But right now I'm trembling, just a little. I'm about to witness the end of a human life, totally arbitrarily, exactly as I decided, in the place I decided. There's nothing else like it. Tomorrow I'm leaving the country for a while. There's still a lot to do. I've got to keep expanding."

I knew that he was right beside me but somehow his voice seemed a long way off.

"Now you're going to die wondering what happened to your life, just like the nobleman's boy. Cheerless, wretched. No one ever comes into this alley. It's over for you."

He moved slightly.

"I bet you don't even know why you're being killed, why this is happening. Life is a mystery. But listen. Why did

I turn up in your life in the first place? Do you believe in fate? Was your fate controlled by me, or was being controlled by me your fate? But in the end, aren't they just two sides of the same coin?"

And with that Kizaki left, stepping on me as he passed. I was aware of the bustle and the stifling atmosphere of the crowded street nearby. I sensed a shadow passing, and soon I could no longer hear his footsteps.

Slumped with my back against the wall, I used my hands to stem the slow trickle of blood. As my vision blurred and the pain increased, I thought about how I didn't want to die. I didn't want it to end like this. Images of the boy, of Ishikawa and Saeko, flashed through my mind.

It was like I could see myself still working a crowd. Roaming here and there, stealing people's wallets—maybe I could even go abroad. London, for example, is still supposed to have a culture of artful pickpockets. Perhaps I could pit my skills against theirs. The world is full of stupid rich people and it would be fun to keep taking their money. Outside the alley, in a misty place far beyond, I could see the tower. It was still standing there, high and remote. I could steal from the rich all over the world and give the money to street kids. I imagined the warm tingling in my fingertips. To press forward as a pickpocket, to become a true pickpocket, I would continue until I dissolved and crumbled into the crowd like sparks.

Yes, that's it, I thought to myself.

And then I heard footsteps far in the distance. Someone was crossing the street outside the alley. I heard young women's voices, chatting busily, complaining about work and customers. It was quite a long way to the entrance to the passage, but if I could hit them with something they would notice me. There were no stones around me, my coat had been taken and I didn't have the strength to take off my shoes. In my trouser pocket, however, I found a coin.

It was a 500 yen piece. I must have taken it from someone's pocket without realizing. I had no idea when. I grinned weakly. If my hands searched for money spontaneously, I must be a proper pickpocket. If I could hit someone with this blood-stained coin they'd be bound to look in my direction.

That bastard took pickpockets too lightly, I thought, listening to the footsteps coming closer. I was damned if I was going to die here. Surely my life hadn't been so pointless I deserved a death like this. With all my strength I squeezed the coin in my fingers. Far off, standing tall, was the hazy tower.

When I spied the figure of a person I hurled the coin, grimacing with pain. The bloody disc blotted out the sun's rays, glistening darkly in the air, as though hoping for some kind of deviation.

Sources

Maurer, David W. *Whiz Mob: A Correlation of the Technical Argot of Pickpockets with Their Behavior Pattern*. Rowman & Littlefield. 1964.

Pickpocket. Dir. Robert Bresson. Perf. Martin LaSalle and Marika Green. Compagnie Cinématographique de France. 1959.

Yeager, Wayne B. *Techniques of the Professional Pickpocket*. Breakout Productions, Inc. 1990.

Other Titles in the Soho Crime Series

David Downing cont.
(World War I)
Jack of Spies
One Man's Flag
Lenin's Roller Coaster
The Dark Clouds Shining

Agnete Friis
(Denmark)
What My Body Remembers

Leighton Gage
(Brazil)
Blood of the Wicked
Buried Strangers
Dying Gasp
Every Bitter Thing
A Vine in the Blood
Perfect Hatred
The Ways of Evil Men

Michael Genelin
(Slovakia)
Siren of the Waters
Dark Dreams
The Magician's Accomplice
Requiem for a Gypsy

Timothy Hallinan
(Thailand)
The Fear Artist
For the Dead
The Hot Countries
Fools' River

(Los Angeles)
Crashed
Little Elvises
The Fame Thief
Herbie's Game
King Maybe
Fields Where They Lay

Karo Hämäläinen
(Finland)
Cruel Is the Night

Mette Ivie Harrison
(Mormon Utah)
The Bishop's Wife
His Right Hand
For Time and All Eternities

Mick Herron
(England)
Down Cemetery Road
The Last Voice You Hear
Reconstruction
Smoke and Whispers
Why We Die
Slow Horses
Dead Lions
Nobody Walks
Real Tigers
Spook Street
This Is What Happened

**Lene Kaaberbøl &
Agnete Friis**
(Denmark)
The Boy in the Suitcase
Invisible Murder
Death of a Nightingale
The Considerate Killer

Heda Margolius Kovály
(1950s Prague)
Innocence

Martin Limón
(South Korea)
Jade Lady Burning
Slicky Boys
Buddha's Money
The Door to Bitterness
The Wandering Ghost
G.I. Bones
Mr. Kill
The Joy Brigade
Nightmare Range
The Iron Sickle
The Ville Rat
Ping-Pong Heart
The Nine-Tailed Fox

Ed Lin
(Taiwan)
Ghost Month
Incensed

Peter Lovesey
(England)
The Circle
The Headhunters

Peter Lovesey cont.
False Inspector Dew
Rough Cider
On the Edge
The Reaper

(Bath, England)
The Last Detective
Diamond Solitaire
The Summons
Bloodhounds
Upon a Dark Night
The Vault
Diamond Dust
The House Sitter
The Secret Hangman
Skeleton Hill
Stagestruck
Cop to Corpse
The Tooth Tattoo
The Stone Wife
*Down Among
the Dead Men*
Another One Goes Tonight
Beau Death

(London, England)
Wobble to Death
*The Detective Wore
Silk Drawers*
Abracadaver
Mad Hatter's Holiday
The Tick of Death
A Case of Spirits
Swing, Swing Together
Waxwork

Jassy Mackenzie
(South Africa)
Random Violence
Stolen Lives
The Fallen
Pale Horses
Bad Seeds

Sujata Massey
(1920s Bombay)
*The Widows of
Malabar Hill*

Francine Mathews
(Nantucket)
Death in the Off-Season
Death in Rough Water
Death in a Mood Indigo
Death in a Cold Hard Light
Death on Nantucket

Seichō Matsumoto
(Japan)
*Inspector Imanishi
Investigates*

Magdalen Nabb
(Italy)
Death of an Englishman
Death of a Dutchman
Death in Springtime
Death in Autumn
*The Marshal and
the Murderer*
*The Marshal and
the Madwoman*
The Marshal's Own Case
*The Marshal Makes
His Report*
*The Marshal
at the Villa Torrini*
Property of Blood
Some Bitter Taste
The Innocent
Vita Nuova
The Monster of Florence

Fuminori Nakamura
(Japan)
The Thief
Evil and the Mask
Last Winter, We Parted
The Kingdom
The Boy in the Earth
Cult X

Stuart Neville
(Northern Ireland)
The Ghosts of Belfast
Collusion
Stolen Souls
The Final Silence

Stuart Neville cont.
Those We Left Behind
So Say the Fallen

(Dublin)
Ratlines

Rebecca Pawel
(1930s Spain)
Death of a Nationalist
Law of Return
The Watcher in the Pine
The Summer Snow

Kwei Quartey
(Ghana)
*Murder at Cape
Three Points*
Gold of Our Fathers
Death by His Grace

Qiu Xiaolong
(China)
Death of a Red Heroine
A Loyal Character Dancer
When Red Is Black

John Straley
(Alaska)
*The Woman Who
Married a Bear*
The Curious Eat Themselves
The Big Both Ways
Cold Storage, Alaska

Akimitsu Takagi
(Japan)
The Tattoo Murder Case
Honeymoon to Nowhere
The Informer

Helene Tursten
(Sweden)
Detective Inspector Huss
The Torso
The Glass Devil
Night Rounds
The Golden Calf
The Fire Dance
The Beige Man
The Treacherous Net

Helene Tursten cont.
Who Watcheth
Protected by the Shadows

**Janwillem van de
Wetering**
(Holland)
Outsider in Amsterdam
Tumbleweed
The Corpse on the Dike
Death of a Hawker
The Japanese Corpse
The Blond Baboon
The Maine Massacre
The Mind-Murders
The Streetbird
The Rattle-Rat
Hard Rain
Just a Corpse at Twilight
Hollow-Eyed Angel
The Perfidious Parrot
*The Sergeant's Cat:
Collected Stories*

Timothy Williams
(Guadeloupe)
Another Sun
*The Honest Folk
of Guadeloupe*

(Italy)
Converging Parallels
The Puppeteer
Persona Non Grata
Black August
Big Italy
*The Second Day
of the Renaissance*

Jacqueline Winspear
(1920s England)
Maisie Dobbs
Birds of a Feather